The Certified Health Education Specialist:

A Self-Study Guide for Professional Competency

THIRD EDITION

Michael J. Cleary, Ed.D., CHES
Professor, Slippery Rock University, Slippery Rock, Pennsylvania
Brad L. Neiger, Ph.D., CHES
Associate Professor, Brigham Young University, Provo, Utah

Edited by
Kathleen Middleton, M.S., CHES
Publisher, ToucanEd

Based on an original work by
Sigrid G. Deeds, Dr.P.H., CHES
Professor Emerita, California State University Long Beach,
Long Beach, California

The use of this study guide is not a guarantee of the successful completion of the Certified Health Education Specialist (CHES) examination. Please review the section *How To Use This Book* for a description of the purpose of this resource. Any expectation beyond the purpose stated in this section is solely the responsibility of the user and not that of the National Commission for Health Education Credentialing, Inc.

Published by The National Commission for Health Education Credentialing, Inc.,
944 Marcon Blvd., Suite 310, Allentown, PA 18013
Telephone (610) 264-8200
Fax 1-800-813-0727

ISBN-0-9652570-0-2

TABLE OF CONTENTS

ACKNOWLEDGEMENTS

This book would not be possible without the review and collaboration of many dedicated professionals. The Division Board for Professional Preparation provided guidance and support from the beginning. Specifically, Dr. John Sciacca provided assistance with the research and evaluation sections, and the Executive Director of NCHEC, William B. Cosgrove, provided ongoing guidance and support.

A significant addition to this edition are the new practice questions which have been totally revised, reviewed and designed; this contribtuion was made by the Division Board for Certification of Health Education Specialists.

We wish to thank these professionals for their work:
       Emily Tyler, Coordinator
       William Chen
       Susan Giarratano-Russell
       Gary Gilmore
       Gail Taylor-Rice
       Bruce Uhrich

Thank You,

M.C.
B.N.
K.M.

I N T R O D U C T I O N

PREFACE

In 1992, Sigrid G. Deeds, Dr.P.H., CHES, authored the original edition of *The Health Education Specialist: A Self-Study Guide to Professional Competency* based on 25 years of health education experience in a variety of settings including state and county health departments, voluntary agencies, and medical and the corporate arenas. Because of its success in helping thousands of applicants prepare for the CHES examination, The National Commission for Health Education Credentialing requested Division Board for Professional Preparation directors Michael Cleary, Ed.D., CHES and Brad Neiger, Ph.D., CHES to work with Dr. Deeds to produce a Second Edition that would reflect emerging developments in health education practice as well as recent changes in the CHES examination. Published in 1996, the Second Edition of *The Certified Health Education Specialist: A Self-Study Guide to Professional Competency* subsequently included revised and updated practice questions, some of which were derived (with permission of the Professional Examination Service) from earlier versions of the CHES exam. Also included was the Test Specifications Document which serves as the basis for all CHES examination questions.

The Third Edition (1998) of *The Certified Health Education Specialist: A Self-Study Guide to Professional Competency* has been authored by Drs. Cleary and Neiger and edited by Kathleen Middleton, M.S., CHES. Features include new practice questions that have been carefully reviewed and revised by the Division Board for CHES, updated resources, and an easier-to-read practice question format. As before, the Test Specifications Document is located in the Appendices. These changes necessarily and accurately reflect recent test modifications that will be in effect beginning with the 1998 Spring CHES exam.

How To Use This Book

The purpose of this book is to guide your self-study as you strengthen your skills in and knowledge of the processes of health education and add to your proficiency and professionalism. It is specifically designed to assist your preparation to certify as a Health Education Specialist. Certification provides recognition of your knowledge base in the basic competencies of our profession.

The *Self-Study Guide* can be used effectively by both individuals and groups to prepare for the CHES examination. Individually, you will want to closely review the entire *Self-Study Guide* noting areas where you have identified weaknesses or gaps in your knowledge base of health education. These areas of concern can then be strengthened by the supplemental readings described in the back of the *Self-Study Guide*. In addition, the Test Specifications Document in Appendix II highlights the Knowledge Statements around which the actual exam questions are developed. Feedback from successful CHES applicants indicates that it is also helpful to be part of a small group that "works through" each practice question by discussing why a certain answer is correct or incorrect. Finally, you may want to contact the nearest college or university that has a health education department to determine if any faculty are facilitating a CHES exam review session.

The selection of study material, examples, and practice questions are based on the authors' judgements in collaboration with the Division Board for CHES to ensure relevance to the CHES examination. The practice questions themselves, however, *have not been subjected to vigorous psychometric testing procedures and thus the validity and reliability of the items have not been established.* The correct answers can be found in Appendix III. We also recommend that you consider the questions as opportunities to identify the underlying concepts in the questions as opposed to merely finding the "right" answer. It is strongly recommended that you use the references that appear in the back of the book. This *Self-Study Guide* can not be used in place of original sources. It is intended to be used as a tool with those sources.

OUTLINE
The Context of Health Education

Key Practice
Questions

1. Which one of the following components in the Health Field Concept has the <u>least</u> impact on health status?
    a) Health Care
    b) Human biology
    c) Environment
    d) Lifestyle behaviors

2. According to the Surgeon General's Report, **Healthy People 2000**, which has the greatest potential for decreasing morbidity?
    a) Human biology
    b) Environment
    c) Lifestyle behaviors
    d) Health care

3. **Healthy People 2000** categorizes U.S. health issues according to:
    a) Primary, secondary, and tertiary prevention
    b) Health promotion, protection, and prevention,
    c) Stages of development and health problems from infants to elderly
    d) Morbidity and disability in regions of the U.S.

4. Based on your review of the graph (Figure 1) on page 5, "Infectious and Chronic Disease Rates, U.S. 1900-1970", which one of the following was a major contributor to the death rate in the U.S. at the turn of the century?
    a) Stroke
    b) Heart disease
    c) Cancer
    d) Tuberculosis

5. Two communities have the same crude death rate (8.7 per 1000). Select the correct statement from the following:
    a) Both communities will have similar age-adjusted death rates.
    b) Both communities will have approximately equal numbers of Latino deaths.
    c) If one community has more elderly people than the other, it should have a higher crude death rate.
    d) Adding sex and age-specific distributions would make it possible to study differences in the communities.

6. Which of the following graphs (A, B, C, or D) reflects a measles epidemic?
   a) A
   b) B
   c) C
   d) D

7. Which of the following graphs (A, B, C, or D) could reflect endemic rabies in this community?
   a) A
   b) B
   c) C
   d) D

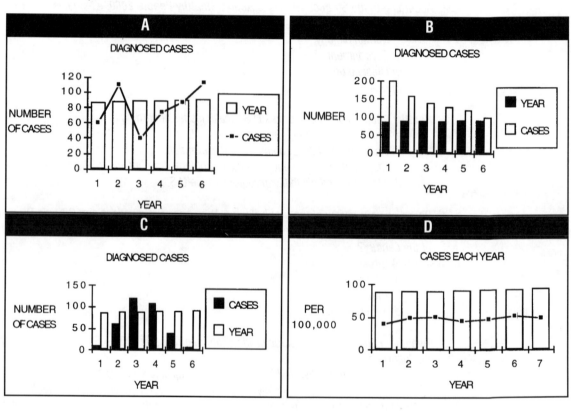

8. Which of the following techniques is an example of secondary prevention?
   a) Mammography
   b) Immunization
   c) Cardiac rehabilitation
   d) Smoking cessation

9. The phrase "excess deaths" expresses the difference between the number of deaths observed in a group and the number expected if the death rates were similar to the general population. Based on the last several years of data, select the correct statement from the following:
    a) Excess deaths for infant mortality among African-Americans are four times higher than for Caucasians.
    b) Excess deaths due to unintentional injuries are lower for African-American males aged 18-25 years than for females aged 18-25 years.
    c) Excess deaths of African-Americans occur mostly after age 65.
    d) The major contributors to excess deaths for African-American males are cancer and infectious diseases.

10. Which one of the following is the correct rank for unintentional injury as a cause for age-specific mortality for individuals 15-24 years of age in the U.S. in recent years?
    a) First
    b) Second
    c) Third
    d) Fourth

11. Of the following, the disease that has caused the most deaths in United States residents aged 45-64 in recent years is:
    a) Diabetes
    b) Heart disease
    c) Cancer
    d) Stroke

12. Which one of the following statistics is the most used in routinely comparing the health status of regions, states and countries?
    a) Infant mortality rate
    b) Neonatal death rate
    c) Fetal mortality rate
    d) Perinatal mortality rate

13. The adult learner responds more to:
    a) Traditional lectures
    b) Problem-solving experiences
    c) Role-playing experiences
    d) Self-study reading assignments

THE CONTEXT OF HEALTH EDUCATION

The last responsibility listed, Communicating, *(see Appendix II, page 101)* comprises three competencies that set the context for the entire outline. Health education does not occur in a vacuum. It is important for you to know the social, political, and economic context of our society, both past and current, that shaped our professional history and shapes our actions as well as our assumptions about health and disease. Therefore, we have put this responsibility at the beginning to give it the importance it deserves and to set the stage for the processes.

VII. COMMUNICATE HEALTH AND HEALTH EDUCATION NEEDS, CONCERNS, AND RESOURCES

- *Keep abreast of professional literature, current trends, and research.*
- *Advocate for inclusion of health education in programs and services.*
- *Explain the foundations of the discipline of health education, including its purposes, theories, history, ethics, and contributions, to promote the development and practice of health education.*

A. HEALTH NEEDS AND CONCERNS

- HEALTH PRIORITIES IN 1996
    1. The ten major causes of death in the U.S. *(see Table 1, page 10)*
    2. Year 2000: Objectives for the Nation *(see reference page 119)*
    3. The need for prevention. Focus has moved from the '70s physician/medical care capacity building and the '80s individual health promotion/wellness emphasis to community/environmental forces, resource allocation/quality of life issues related to prevention and promotion in the '90s, equity, and justice.

- FORCES SHAPING HEALTH TODAY
    1. Shift from acute to chronic diseases and theory of multicausality *(see Figure 1, page 5)*
    2. Costs
    3. Medical technology
    4. Demographics — population size, percentages, change-aging and immigration
    5. Telecommunications
    6. Media advocacy and social marketing
    7. Health care reform

- TOOLS FOR COMMUNITY HEALTH STUDY
    1. Epidemiology — study of determinants and distribution of diseases in human populations (person, place, time). Determine causality and association.

**Figure 1
INFECTIOUS AND
CHRONIC DISEASE
DEATH RATES IN THE
U.S. 1900-1970**

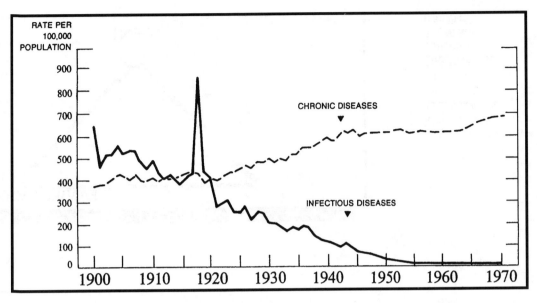

**Figure 2
LEVELS OF
PREVENTION**
This diagram from
Pickett and Hanlon
(Pickett, 1990)
shows the relationship
of the levels of
prevention to the stages
of disease, impairment,
disability, and
dependency.

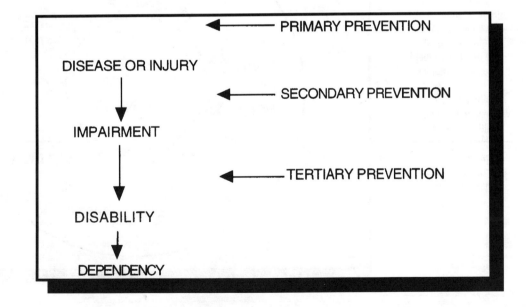

Figure 3
FACTORS IN THE CONTROL OF INFECTIOUS DISEASES
Infectious diseases are controlled by intervening at one of these three points.

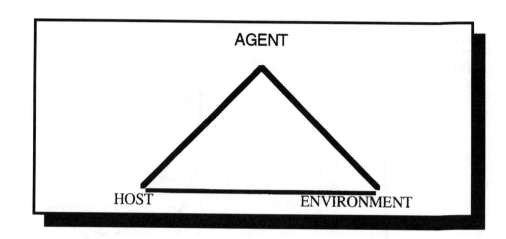

Figure 4
FACTORS AFFECTING INDIVIDUALS' HEALTH
Agencies and individuals have different views about the amount of influence each of these factors has on the health of an individual (e.g., the CDC attributes over 50% of the effect to lifestyle, whereas many public health field workers think that social, cultural, and physical environment rate the largest share of the attribution).

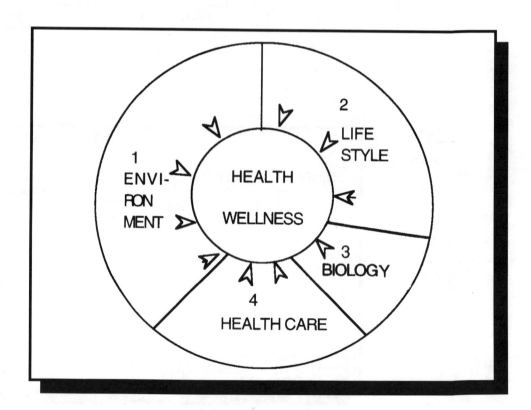

    2. Demography — study of human populations — size, composition, distribution, density, growth, etc., and origins of change. *(See page 12 for public health concepts.)*

- FACTORS AFFECTING INDIVIDUAL HEALTH STATUS
  1. Environment
  2. Lifestyle
  3. Biology — genetics, aging
  4. Access to health care

- DETERMINANTS OF INEQUITY IN HEALTH STATUS OF GROUPS
  1. Ethnicity
  2. Location
  3. Income
  4. Age
  5. Education
  6. Occupation
  7. Acculturation

- THE PLAYERS IN THE HEALTH FIELD
  1. Major international agencies
  2. Government agencies — federal, state, local
  3. Major voluntary agencies
  4. National health education associations
  5. Managed Care Organizations
  6. Hospitals

B. INTERPRET CONCEPTS, PURPOSES, THEORIES OF HEALTH EDUCATION PROCESS

- CHARACTERISTICS OF HEALTH EDUCATION
  1. Definitions *(see page 9)*
     a. Process
     b. Outcome
  2. Foundations of health education are educational, biological, behavioral, sociological sciences, and public health
  3. Learner/client-oriented philosophy and ethics
  4. Prevention and health promotion-oriented
  5. Intangible — therefore, heavy emphasis on evaluation/accountability
  6. Scarce resources — therefore, focus on efficiency and effectiveness
  7. Professionalism

- PHILOSOPHY, PRINCIPLES, ETHICS OF HEALTH EDUCATION
    See page 15

- HISTORY
    See page 8

- THEORIES
    See page 68

C. ADVOCATE FOR INCLUSION OF HEALTH EDUCATION

Community or social advocacy is a process used for social change. This process includes community organizing, coalition building, and education of the community and its decision makers. Technical assistance and consultation may be used to build the capacity of community members and groups to address health issues and influence social change.

Health education advocates recognize and address barriers that impede successful health education interventions, promote self-help, community participation, capacity building, and health behavior change, and show sensitivity to the needs of diverse populations. *(Standards of Practice, 1991)*

Advocacy for health education also requires knowing the successes in the field, the effectiveness of interventions, and the conditions required to achieve successful behavior change.

HISTORY OF U.S. SCHOOL AND PUBLIC HEALTH EDUCATION

1798...
U.S. Public Health Service begun as the Merchant Marine Hospital Service

Local health departments:
Baltimore, 1878
Charleston, 1815
Philadelphia, 1818

1837...
First of Horace Mann's Annual Reports campaigned for mandatory programs of hygiene

1850-1900...
1850 Lemuel Shattuck authored "Report of the Sanitary Commission of Massachusetts," aka "The Shattuck Report"

1866 Stephen Smith, a physician, and Dorman E. Eaton, a lawyer, wrote Magna Carta for health departments. Their methods: gathered facts, urged backing of medical profession, popular support, and legislative action

The Certified Health Education Specialist

HEALTH EDUCATION DEFINITIONS

There are dozens of definitions of health education. The first one that follows was chosen because it was developed in the role delineation project that grew into the current credentialing process.

DEFINITION ONE
Health education is the process of assisting individuals, acting separately and collectively, to make informed decisions on matters affecting individual, family, and community health. Based upon scientific foundations, health education is a field of interest, a discipline, a profession.
The Role Delineation Process

The second one focuses on the important elements of the health education program process: designed (planned, not accidental) combination of methods (use more than one to be effective); voluntary (participants have choices) adaptations (we may wish to prevent, initiate, or sustain existing behavior, not just change) of behavior.

DEFINITION TWO
Health education is any designed combination of methods to facilitate voluntary adaptations of behavior conducive to health.
Green et al., Health Education Planning

1869 Massachusetts forms first true State Board of Health

Louis Pasteur discoveries from **1870-72**

State health depts. started: Louisiana Health Dept.

1855 Yellow fever epidemic: Massachusetts, 1869 Washington, D.C., 1870 California and Virginia, 1871

Health departments focused on sanitation, control of epidemics, quarantine, fumigation, legal and policy issues

Rapid growth of school health education, stimulated by Mann's writings, growth of voluntary agencies, child study movement, and pubic health

Early 1900s...
Rise of health departments

1901 Thomas D. Wood, M.D., "Father of health education" established program of professional preparation in hygiene at Columbia University

First of White House conferences on the health of children

1902 Public Health Service Act organized Public Health and Merchant Marine Hospital Service, renamed U.S. Public Health Service in 1912

Table 1
TEN LEADING CAUSES
OF DEATH IN THE
UNITED STATES
National Center
for Health Statistics,
1995

Cause of Death	Percentage of Total	Risk Factors
Heart disease	31.8%	Smoking, hypertension, hypercholesterolemia, lack of exercise, diabetes mellitus, obesity, stress
Cancer	23.2%	Smoking, alcohol, diet, environmental carcinogens, obesity
Stroke	6.8%	Hypertension, smoking, hypercholesterolemia, stress
Chronic obstructive lung disease	4.4%	Smoking
Injuries	4.0%	Alcohol and other drugs, failure to use seat belts, speeding, access to guns
Pneumonia and influenza	3.5%	Smoking, alcohol
Diabetes mellitus	2.5%	Obesity
AIDS	1.8%	Unsafe sex
Suicide	1.3%	Stress, alcohol, drug use, depression
Chronic liver disease & cirrhosis	1.1%	Alcohol
Other	19.7%	
All causes	100%	Total Deaths = 2,313,132

1911 Creation of Joint Committee on Health Problems in Education (NEA and AMA)

1917 Involvement of the learner in the learning process

1918 American Child Health Association established to improve the health of children

Voluntary health agencies (1918, National TB Association; now American Lung Association)

Sally Lucas Jeans started health campaigns, some efforts in public schools

New knowledge gained by Kock, Lister discoveries

The public health educators were writers, journalists, social workers, and nurses (home visits) focused on communicable diseases, infant and maternal mortality, poor sanitary conditions.

School health education included in professional training programs in normal schools

Many babies died of communicable diseases/poor nutrition

1920s...

1921 Mary Spencer, first student to complete all three degree programs in health education, was awarded Ph.D. by Columbia University

SCHOOL HEALTH EDUCATION CONCEPTS

Health education is an applied science basic to the general education of all children and youth. Its body of knowledge represents a synthesis of facts, principles, and concepts drawn from biological, behavioral, sociological, and health sciences, but interpreted in terms of human needs, human values, and human potential. Acquisition of information is a desired purpose but not the primary goal of instruction. Rather, growth in critical thinking ability and problem-solving skills are both the process and the product of instruction. The ultimate goal of health education is the development of an adult whose lifestyle reflects actions that tend to promote his or her own health as well as that of the family and the community.

School health starts from a developmental point of view of keeping healthy children healthy and giving them command of health knowledge and skills, using the individual or the classroom as the unit of analysis.

Public health, on the other hand, focuses on populations, the community, and organizations. It starts from a health problem point of view and assumes that the environment, social and political as well as physical, is a major aspect of ameliorating a problem. *(Pollock, 1992)*

The Comprehensive School Health model has classically been a triad consisting of health services, health education, and a healthful environment. The model has been extended to include physical education, school counseling and social services, food service, faculty and staff wellness, and integrated school, family, and community involvement, making eight interactive components. *(Allensworth, 1987) (Kolbe, 1995)*

1921 MIT Health education training under Professor Claire Turner & W.T. Sedgwick, M.D. at Harvard-MIT. Started first MPH program; conducted Summerville and Malden Studies to clarify the status and role of health education

1922 Public Health Education Section of APHA founded. Lecture, information giving, the beginning of the use of advertising

1925 School health movement– school nurses hygiene education– physical examinations

Metropolitan Life Insurance Co.– Community nurses to help people take care of themselves.

Yale and North Carolina Schools of Public Health introduced a course or major in health education

1930s...

1930 The beginning of the use of community organization; use of existing community groups — their resources and relationships (e.g., PTA, voluntary agencies)

1931 The Cattagaugus Study, directed by Ruth Grout, studied the impact of health education and the competency of health teachers

1935 Social Security Act passed

PUBLIC HEALTH CONCEPTS

<u>PREVENTION:</u> Definition: Anticipatory action taken to reduce the possibility of an event or condition occurring or developing, or to minimize the damage that may result from the event or condition if it does occur. *(Torjman: Prevention in the drug field. 1. Essential concepts and strategies. Toronto, Addiction Research Foundation, 1986)*

<u>Primary prevention</u> Strategies to reduce the incidence of cases: 1) make the host stronger and more resistant; 2) decrease the effect of the agent upon the host; 3) create a barrier in the environment.

<u>Secondary prevention</u> Objective is to reduce prevalence. Methods are screening and casefinding for early detection, diagnosis, and treatment to limit disability.

<u>Tertiary prevention</u> Objective is to slow progress of disease or avoid other complications of the disease process. Aim to reduce impact of existing conditions on the Quality of Life (QOL).
(Adapted from Pickett, 1991)

See Figures 2 and 3 on pages 5 and 6.

EPIDEMIOLOGICAL TERMS:

<u>Incidence</u> The number of new cases occurring during a defined time.

<u>Prevalence</u> The number of cases in the community (state, world, etc.) at a given time.

<u>Excess deaths</u> The difference between the number of deaths observed in a group and the number expected if the death rates were similar to the general population.

1936 The Astoria Study was directed by Dorothy Nyswander. All aspects of school health programs focusing on school health services

1940s...
Addition of behavioral science theory and inter-personal process to curriculum.
Specialities of schools: North Carolina, community organization; Minnesota and Michigan, school health;

Univeristy of Californa Berkley, behavioral science and processes

1940 Community organization demonstrations in North Carolina around war efforts and needs of workers (communicable diseases).

Beginning of patient education on syphillis and gonorrhea — rapid treatment

1942-1963 Mayhew Derryberry,

Chief of Health Ed. Services (Ph.D. in psychology), helped develop training in behavioral theory and change

1943 School Comm. Health Project in Michigan demonstrated effectiveness of comprehensive school community health program

1944 Similar program demonstrated in California

The Certified Health Education Specialist

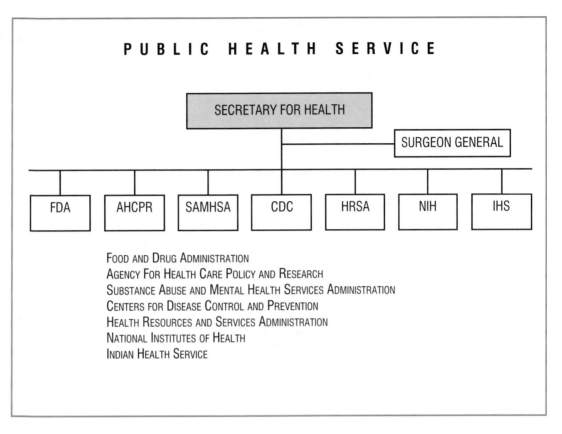

PUBLIC HEALTH SERVICE

SECRETARY FOR HEALTH

SURGEON GENERAL

FDA | AHCPR | SAMHSA | CDC | HRSA | NIH | IHS

Food and Drug Administration
Agency For Health Care Policy and Research
Substance Abuse and Mental Health Services Administration
Centers for Disease Control and Prevention
Health Resources and Services Administration
National Institutes of Health
Indian Health Service

1945 The Denver Interest Study, a needs assessment for the development of curriculum, was conducted

Definition of manpower for the Health Department local units:
Haven Emerson (Yale)
Ira Hiscock (Yale)
Beginnings of research efforts

Proliferation of health education training programs in schools of public health:

1) UNC, Lucy Morgan (community organization)
2) Michigan, Mable Rugen (school)
3) Minnesota, Ruth Grout (school/community)
4) UCB, Dorothy Nyswander (community and interpersonal processes)

Now had 25 accredited schools of public health

1946 World War II officially

ended

1947 460 employed as health educators. 300 had completed graduate courses in recognized schools of public health. (This estimate does not include school or college health educators, PHNs, dentists, etc.)

1948 National Conference on Undergraduate Professional Preparation in Health, Physical Education and Recreation

Crude death rate The total number of deaths at all ages in the jurisdiction for the year divided by the total number of people in the population at midpoint for that year (usually multiplied by 1000).

Age-specific death rates are defined as the deaths among residents (age X) in a specific year divided by the population of the same age at midyear.

Example:

$$\frac{\text{deaths of children 1-5 in California in 1985}}{\text{total \# of children age 1-5 in California at midyear}} \times 1000$$

Screening Use of a test to separate a population segment into two groups: one with a higher-than-average chance of having or developing a specific disease or condition and the other with a lower-than-average chance.

High-risk group Population with a higher-than-average chance of having or developing a specific disease or condition.

Risk factors Characteristics or behavioral patterns that increase a person's risk of disease or disorders (particularly heart disease, stroke, cancer). Risk factors can be divided into those that cannot be modified (age, sex, family history) and those that can (e.g., blood serum cholesterol level, cigarette smoking, high blood pressure).

identified competencies needed by the health educator

1949 First U.S. Office of Education Conference on Undergrad Professional Preparation of Students majoring in health education directed by H.F. Kilander

1950s...
Society of Public Health Educators – Dr. Clair Turner, first president – Fifty charter members. Membership stayed at 500-600 until 1960's

1950 The National Conference on Graduate Study in Health, Physical Education and Recreation established guidelines for graduate education

Midcentury –White House Conference on Children and Youth recommended greater emphasis of health education in the school curriculum through adequately prepared teachers

1953 Creation of the U.S. Department of Health, Education, and Welfare.

1954 The School Health Education Evaluation Study in Los Angeles examined effects of comprehensive school health education

THE PHILOSOPHY OF HEALTH EDUCATION

The value systems and philosophical tenets that underlie health education practice envisioned by the National Task Force have become the salient features for a new definition of what it means to be a competent professional. This new breed of professional must come with intellectual predispositions that are rigorously interdisciplinary, must have an open perspective on human problems, and must have a sense of decency for what it means to be socially conscious. The framework bespeaks the field's deep interest in and collective commitment to codifying and standardizing those core competencies that will be required of a profession that is innovative and responsive to society's ever-changing educational needs for health. No framework can ensure that curricula or other professional development programs will create the "meta" qualities of professional excellence such as dedication, intuitive judgment, motivation, perseverance, caring, or ethical and moral integrity that are vital.

The Code of Ethics for two of the organizations for health education professionals can be found in Responsibilities Section III on implementation.

"Competence" is an expectation that is used to describe clusters of skills and understandings that are recognizable and measurable. The competencies are not fixed, but are open to growth and to change.

"The goal of health education is to promote, maintain, and improve individual and community health. The teaching-learning process is the hallmark and social agenda that differentiates the practice of health education from that of other helping professions in achieving this goal. Like that of the other helping professions, health education's methodologies require its entry into a social contract for dealing with people; however, it is the emphasis on the teaching-learning process — the inherent belief in the individual's capacity to learn and assume responsibility — that comprises the *raison d'etre* of health education and sets it apart from other professions. Health education is eminently committed to enabling an empowered role for people to define their problems, set their priorities, and create practical solutions by which they achieve a sense of interest in, commitment to, and ownership of the

1956 Two college health conferences were chaired by E.B. Johns: the first analyzed health content and methodology; the second studied professional preparation of school health educators

1958 Interagency Conference on School Health Education recommended effective communication among the various elements involved in health education

1959 Highland Park Conference established commissions to study specific issues (philosophy, health instruction, research, intergroup relationships, and accreditation)

1960s...

1961 School Health Education Study (SHES) surveyed nearly 1 million students nationwide and initiated the writing of a K-12 curriculum directed by E. Sliepcevich

1966 The Committee on Graduate Curriculum in Health Education offered recommendations for a core curriculum that included health science, behavioral science education, and research

1969 Teach Us What We Want to Know, a needs and interest survey of 5,000 Connecticut students directed by Ruth Byler

efforts used to address health issues. Health education respects the individual as an actively involved learner and a full partner in the change process who is learning to act on, respond to and improve his or her environment." *(Framework 1996, page 2)*

PRINCIPLES OF HEALTH EDUCATION

Participation is a basic principle. People affected by the problem must be involved in defining the problem, planning and implementing steps to resolve the problem, and establishing structures to ensure that desired change is maintained. This promotes ownership, meaning that local people must have a sense of responsibility for, and control over, the program, promoting change so that they will continue to support the changes. *(Bracht, 1990)*

Participation enables the change program to be designed and adapted to the wide range of learning experiences and current circumstances that affect the group. *(See also Community Settings section.)*

The process of obtaining health behavior through participation and informed consent is the essence of health education. *(Green, 1978, page 29)* The overwhelming weight of evidence is that the durability of behavioral changes is proportional to the degree of active rather than passive participation of the learner. *(Green, 1978, page 34)* *(Roccella, 1984, page 240)*

Empowerment is another basic principle imbuing community residents with understanding of their ability to affect social, economic, and political as well as personal forces. Interventions can provide individuals and communities with a sense of competence and build capacity to change other and future problems. This sense of efficacy has been shown to contribute to changes in health outcome. *(Wallerstein, 1994)*

Cultural sensitivity is a third principle of health education that is basic in changing behavior. As a comprehensive system of beliefs and behaviors, culture provides a powerful framework for understanding the world. *(Davis, 1994)* Communities exhibit distinctive cultures based on these as

1970s...

Major focus on physician/medical care system — access and cost containment

Two branches of health education, school health education and public health education, had grown independently of each other. A dialogue between organizations representing the two branches began to grow

1971 Officially changed title to Society for Public Health Education but retained SOPHE acronym and logo. Stated purpose was "to promote, encourage, and contribute to the health of all people by encouraging study, improving practices, and elevating standards in the field of health education"

Strong state health education programs — California, Pennsylvania, North Carolina, Massachusetts

1971 Coalition of National Health Education Organizations – Members: AAHE, SSDHPER, ACHA, SOPHE, APHA-PHES, CSTDPHE, APHA-SHS, ASHA

1972 The President's Committee on Health Education under President Nixon. Subcommittee on Patient Education

1974 PL 93-641 National Health Planning and Resources

well as historical, geopolitical, and economic dynamics. Failure to understand differences can result in poor use of health services, lack of cooperation, and general alienation of individuals and families from the health care system. *(Nidorf, 1987)* Health education programs have demonstrated the efficacy of culturally appropriate activities. *(Jemmott, 1992)* The groups' skills, economic and environmental impacts of changes, policies, and perceptions of power are all examples of aspects of a thorough assessment.

Standards drive excellence as we have discovered in working with **Objectives for the Nation** these past decades. The school health educators have now produced a set of educational standards that point the way to achieving "health literacy."

National Standards for Health Education (1995)

The goal of these standards is to provide a framework for schools to use to create an instructional program that will enable the students to become healthy and capable of academic success.

Health literacy is the capacity of individuals to obtain, interpret, and understand basic health information and services in ways that enhance health.

S T A N D A R D S

1. Students will comprehend concepts related to health promotion and disease prevention.
2. Students will demonstrate the ability to access valid health information and health-promoting products and services.
3. Students will demonstrate the ability to practice health-enhancing behaviors and reduce health risks.
4. Students will analyze the influence of culture, media, technology, and other factors on health.
5. Students will demonstrate the ability to use interpersonal communication skills to enhance health.
6. Students will demonstrate the ability to use goal-setting and decision-making skills to enhance health.
7. Students will demonstrate the ability to advocate for personal, family, and community health. *(NHES, 1995)*

Development Act. Federal focus established Bureau of Health Education in CDC

1976 94-317 National Consumer Health Information and Health Promotion Act

OHIP Office of the Surgeon General – PHS – HHS

1977 National Center for Health Education

1978 National Center for Health Education facilitated the Role Delineation Project

Office of Comprehensive School Health within the Department of Education created by PL 95-561

Conference on The Commonalities and Differences in the Preparation and Practice of Health Educators held in Bethesda, Maryland

1979 Healthy People: The Surgeon General's Report on Health Promotion and Disease Prevention

1980s...
Focus on health promotion/wellness for individuals

1985 The Initial Role Delineation for Health Education, Final Report published

PROGRAM DESIGN FOUNDATIONS:

The first task in changing behavior is to determine its characteristics by a needs assessment and then systematically develop a variety of interventions as resources allow based on theory, data, and participation. Behavior has multiple bases, so we need multiple methods to effect change.

Interventions are educational rather than coercive or manipulative and consist of education, training, resource development, and rewards. First things first. Interventions and their subsumed learning experiences usually have a logical developmental sequence and should build on the experience that the learner already has. As much as possible, adapt learning experiences to each individual. When that is not possible in large-scale programs, provide self-help and review materials and feedback mechanisms. Immediate feedback helps learners adapt to new ideas.

There is no built-in superiority or inferiority in any method of intervention to achieve behavioral change. It depends on the circumstances, the target audience, the timing, and the enthusiasm and commitment of the change agent. *(Adapted from Green, 1991)*

The effectiveness of specific interventions depends on their appropriate selection and application. Predictive of effectiveness are reinforcement, feedback, individualization, facilitation, and relevance. *(Mullen, 1990)*

CONDITIONS THAT FACILITATE LEARNING:

A situation that encourages people to be active, promoting each individual's discovery of the personal meaning of ideas; that emphasizes the uniquely personal and subjective nature of learning and that difference is good and desirable; that people have a right to make mistakes; that displays tolerance of ambiguity; a cooperative process with emphasis on self-evaluation; that encourages openness of self; that permits confrontation; that encourages learners to trust themselves as well as external sources; where people feel respected and accepted.

1987 AAHE Directory lists 317 professional preparation programs in school and community health education

1988 Establishment of National Commission for Health Education Credentialing, Inc.

1990s...
Focus on impact of environmental/policy issues on health and distributive justice

1990 First examination for Certified Health Education Specialist (CHES)

Healthy People 2000 sets national health promotion and prevention priorities. Includes health education for first time

1994 The School Health Policies and Programs Study (SHPPS) conducted by the CDC provides in-depth description of school health programs at state, district,

school, and classroom levels.

1995 National Health Education Standards for students are developed by the Joint Committee on National Health Education Standards

3400 active CHES are listed on the NHEC roles

AAHE Directory lists 210 professional preparation programs in school, communitiy, and public

ADULT EDUCATION CONCEPTS:

Andragogy, the art and science of teaching adults, is based on a set of assumptions about learning that is different from traditional pedagogy. The four main assumptions are:

Changes in self-concept: As a person matures his self-concept moves from one of total dependency (as an infant) to increasing self-directedness.

Experience: Increasing use of experiential techniques as the growing reservoir of experience of an adult causes him to be an expanding and richer resource for learning. This conveys a respect for the adult as a unique individual.

Readiness to learn: Assumption that learners are ready to learn those things they "need" because of the development phases that are approaching in their multiple roles. This contrasts with the pedagogical approach of providing what "ought" to be learned. The critical implication here is the importance of timing learning experiences to coincide with learners' developmental tasks.

Orientation to learning: The adult's is a problem-centered orientation to learning instead of subject-centered orientation. It differs from a child's learning in that a child's learning is one of postponed application vs. the adult learning emphasis on immediacy of application. *(Knowles, 1980)*

health education

1996 SOPHE HQ moves to Washington, D.C.

NCHEC HQ moves to Allentown, Pennsylvania

Joint Committee for Graduate Standards convenes a national congress in Dallas, Texas to finalize and validate the competencies of a graduate-level health educator

1997 A consensus statement on standards and assessment for school health education and physical education was released by the Society of State Directors of Health, Physical Education and Recreation

A meeting convened by SSDHPER, involved CDC/DASH, AAHE, CCSSO and NASPE.

SOME EXAMPLES OF EFFECTIVE HEALTH EDUCATION

Farquhar, J.W., S.P. Fortmann, J.A. Flora, et al. "Effects of Community-Wide Education on Cardiovascular Disease Risk Factors—The Stanford 5-City Project." <u>JAMA</u> 264 (1990): 359-65.

Puska, P. N. Aulikki, et al. "The Community-Based Strategy to Prevent Coronary Heart Disease: Conclusions from the Ten Years of the North Karelia Project." <u>Annual Review Public Health</u> 6 (1985): 147-93.

Morisky, D.L., D.M. Levine, L.W. Green, et al. "Five-Year Blood Pressure Control and Mortality Following Health Education for Hypertensive Patients." <u>AJPH</u> 73 (1983): 153-62.

Garraway, W.M. and J.P. Whisnant. "The Changing Pattern of Hypertension and the Declining Incidence of Stroke." <u>JAMA</u> 258 (1987): 214-17.

Bertera, R.L. "Planning and Implementing Health Promotion in the Workplace: A Case Study of the DuPont Company Experience." <u>Health Education Quarterly</u> 17 (Fall 1990): 307-327.

I. Assessing Individual and Community Needs for Health Education

1. If you were starting an AIDS program and wanted to know which group to target, which statistics would you use?
   a) Cause-specific mortality data
   b) Cumulative mortality data
   c) Age-specific mortality data
   d) Hospital emergency utilization

2. A local health department wants you, the health education specialist, to help develop a school-based health clinic. The local school board is opposed. Which technique would you use to initiate a productive dialogue?
   a) Focus group
   b) Delphi approach
   c) Nominal group process
   d) Force field analysis.

3. The best demographic predictor for individual success in community-based health education programs is:
   a) Ethnicity
   b) Age
   c) Gender
   d) Education

4. Which one of the following rates provides the number of live births in a population of women aged 15-44 years?
   a) Crude birth rate
   b) General fertility rate
   c) General natality rate
   d) Population natality rate

5. The first step in identifying the need for community health education programs should be to:
   a) Assess existing individual behaviors
   b) Establish program objectives
   c) Conduct a community analysis
   d) Determine the poverty level

6. Which one of the following data sets is the most appropriate to use in determining the level of a community's health status?
   a) Vital statistics
   b) Social and political data
   c) Business and commerce data
   d) Demographic profiles

- *Assess environmental, individual and group characteristics to identify health needs, interests, and concerns.*
- *Assess resources to determine the feasibility of a health education program.*

Needs assessment is a systematic, planned collection of information about the reported needs of individuals or groups. It provides the logical starting point for program planning and for action providing the scientific and political base for program planning. It is the basis for sound planning and eliciting participant buy-in. It is basically a data collection endeavor coupled with the process of target group or community participation. It is linked with the process of determining and ranking priorities but is separate and distinct. Needs assessment is an indispensable tool for priority rating, but ultimately, priority determination exercises are colored by political and value judgments.

Needs assessment is an integral part of the program planning process. One author breaks needs assessment at the community level into analysis and diagnosis. Community analysis is data gathering with the involvement of citizens on the backdrop, health status, health care system and social assistance system. Community diagnosis is the synthesis of all information collected to identify gaps or problems between health status and the provision of health services within the area. *(Dignan, 1987)*

A. GATHER HEALTH-RELATED DATA — Use multiple methods

    1. Sources of Data

        Community Health Status

            Vital Statistics, Local Records (injury, hospitalization, police)

        Community Health Care System — manpower, service delivery

        Community Social Assistance System

        Geographic and Physical Identifiers

        Business and Commerce

        Demographic Characteristics

        Social, Cultural and Political Structure

        State and Federal

            Records, reportable diseases (morbidity, mortality)

            Special Surveys e.g., NHIS, NHHANES

            Epidemiological Studies

        Literature

    2. Data Collection Tools *(see page 26)*

        Community

            Resource Inventory

            Social Indicators

            Key Informant Approach

            Community Forum

            Public Hearings

            Structured Groups — focus, nominal, Delphi panel

            Survey — methods and techniques

School
>
> Cumulative Record
> Standardized Tests and Psychometric Tests
> Screening
> Interviews (teachers, parents, school nurses)
> Surveys

Health-Care Setting
>
> Hospital Admissions and Discharge Data
> Patient Records
> Community Data (see above)
> Interviews and Surveys

Worksite
>
> Health Risk Appraisal/Assessment
> Interviews and Surveys
> Community Data
> Focus Groups

The two types of community analyses are geographical/political and functional. Geopolitical community analysis requires:

1. The map of the service area — political boundaries if applicable
2. Identification and plotting of major health services on the map
3. Total population
4. Age distribution
5. Average household income
6. Main sources of community income
7. Total racial and ethnic distribution in the area
8. Other pertinent information

The functional community analysis requires:

1. Identification of factors that make this a community; profession, ethnicity, work setting or type of condition
2. How can these community members be identified?
3. How can they be accessed in terms of communication?
4. Who are the decision makers or gatekeepers for this group?

Organizations are important for health educators to analyze and understand and take into account in assessment and planning. First, health services are delivered by them, and health programs are shaped by their requirements and constraints. Second, organizing or providing liaison or building coalitions on an interagency basis can be facilitated. Also, health educators with few exceptions are employees whose working environment can promote health and safety or not, and may or may not be amenable to health promotion programs.

Organizational analysis questions:
1. Organization chart (who is in charge? who reports to whom?)
2. Mission of organization and/or statement of philosophy
3. Source of funding
4. Policies of the agency and legal mandates related to your program or project
5. Level of funding for health education
6. Numbers and qualifications of those in charge of health education
7. What are the major health education directions? What health education programs are now in place? Are they competitive/complementary to your plan?
8. At what level will decisions be made about the initiation or continuation of this program?
9. What will be the basis for the decisions about money? public relations? constituent support? community need?
10. Who are the stakeholders in the status quo? Who would benefit or have a piece of the action if new programs are adopted?
11. Who are (will be) the supporters or the detractors of these ideas?
12. Identify the formal and informal communications channels within the organization.

B. ANALYZE INFLUENCES ON HEALTH BEHAVIOR

Each group and its environment is unique; therefore, effective interventions fitted to specific populations require close tailoring based on their knowledge, attitudes, and beliefs. Their culture and the capacity of participants and communities to take health action is important. Culture refers to thoughts, communications, actions, customs, beliefs, values, and institutions of racial, ethnic, religious or social groups. *(Cross, 1989)*

> Knowledge, attitudes, beliefs
> Culture, significant others, environmental factors
> Power — political and economic
> Skills, access to resources
> Economic and environmental impacts
> Policies
> Theories *(see page 68)*

C. ASSESS RESOURCES INCLUDING BARRIERS AND FACILITATORS

> Concerned citizens, stakeholders, competition, collaborators
> Community competence, self-help, resource development
> Analyze policies, resources, and circumstances in the intra-
> or interorganizational situation that can hinder or facilitate
> Tools *(see page 26)*

Framework Requirement

- *Interpret assessment and summarize assessment by analyzing environmental, individual, and group resource data to determine priorities for program development.*

D. INTERPRET NEEDS FOR HEALTH EDUCATION

Analyze data — epidemiological and statistical concepts
Local estimates based on national/state data
Interpret written, graphic, verbal data — use charts, graphs
Compare to local, state, national data, or historical status
Social and attitudinal needs

E. SET PRIORITIES

Criteria: Importance-prevalence, immediacy (urgency),
necessity (must be present for change to occur), changeability

See Hanlon priority list below:

PRIORITY RATING METHOD

Components and Criteria to Consider:

A. Size of the Problem

Percentage of population directly affected

B. Seriousness of the Problem

Urgency — public concern, public health concern

Severity — mortality rates; morbidity, degree and duration; disability, degree and
duration; accessibility, average distance to care and affordability

Medical Costs — individuals directly affected; third-party payers, government costs

Future Needs — potential number who may acquire problem or be affected by
problem; relative degree of complication and involvement

C. Effectiveness of the Solution — How well can the problem be solved?

Defined as improvement of the service or programs offered or in relation to current
services as a result of the implementation of the suggested solution.

CRITERIA CHECKLIST FOR PRIORITIZING HEALTH PROBLEMS *(Hanlon)*

A. Percent of Population Affected
B. Economical Loss
C. Loss of Manpower (productivity)
D. Severity
E. Urgency

F. Medical Costs
G. Future Need
H. Economic Feasibility
I. How Easily Can We Solve This Problem?
J. How Quickly Can We Solve This Problem?
K. Are There Enough Resources?
L. Legality
M. Acceptability
N. Priority

PEARL is an acronym used to remember the Hanlon priorities. It stands for **P**riority, **E**conomic feasibility, **A**cceptability, **R**esources, **L**egality.

NEEDS ASSESSMENT TOOLS

Surveys Complex and expensive. Use to get knowledge, attitudes, beliefs, behavior. Good survey is well constructed, tested for validity, and has high response rate and valid sample. Surveys are reactive and may arouse expectations. Survey formats are mail (cheapest, may have low response rate, only for literate, information is structured and limited), telephone (faster, selective to those with phones, more depth possible), and face-to-face (expensive, can get in-depth responses). Data analysis and report dissemination should be planned at outset.

Unstructured or semi-structured interviews Pros: More opportunity than surveys to discover information, obtain more complete information, especially suited for obtaining valuable info from busy people. Cons: Interviewers need knowledge of the subject of interview (the less interviewer background, the more structured the interview and more training is needed); data analysis is more difficult; these interviews are more costly.

Key informant interviews Key informants are strategically placed individuals who have knowledge and ability to report on the needs of an institution: in a corporation or hospital, or in the community. They are aware of the needs and services perceived by the target as important. Because they are important members, they can affect the support and buy-in for program changes. They may be biased. The full range of community perspective should be reflected in selection. The "snowball" technique where they are asked to recommend others for interviews can provide insights into networks and communicators. Key informant surveys are quick and relatively inexpensive to conduct. A maximum of 10 to 15 questions should cover both general and specific needs of target population, issues of accessibility, and acceptability of solutions. Recommend mail or phone pre-notice that includes an outline of questions and a face-to-face interview.

Resource inventories Use of records and agency interviews can establish who is providing services, what services are provided, comprehensiveness and continuity of service, and where problems and gaps exist.

Observational methods for large-scale studies Outcomes of the target population are measured directly rather than indirectly through self-reports or reports of others. Most of the techniques listed assume that direct observational information is not available or relevant. Like epidemiological surveys, most observational techniques are complicated and require expert consultation.

Community forums A public meeting seeking broad-scale participation to review various perspectives on a particular subject. Pros: Relatively straightforward to conduct, relatively inexpensive, opportunity for all views since it is publicly advertised; people can participate on their own terms; can identify people who are most interested and may later be prepared to participate. Cons: Hard to generate attendance, draws respondents with special interests; can degenerate into complaint session; data analysis may be time-consuming.

Figure 6
FORCE FIELD
ANALYSIS
List the forces that tend to support the status quo and then list the forces that push toward change.

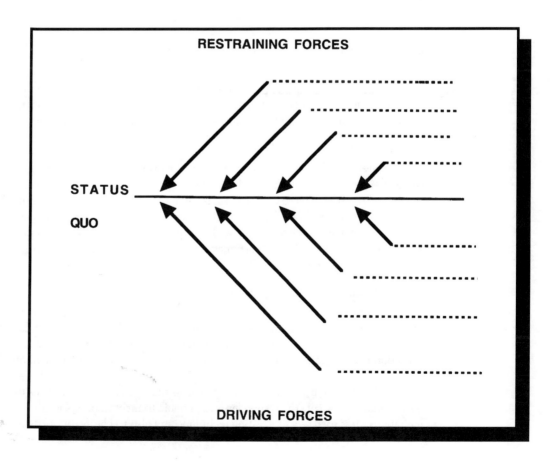

Electronic conferencing Alternative to face-to-face meetings, video, audio, computer teleconferencing slow to develop because of cost and discomfort of participants. Audio less expensive than video but requires more discipline on part of participant to listen and to contribute. Pros: Way to bring widely scattered people together at relatively low cost; way to bring busy people together; can be conducted relatively quickly; individuals not influenced by status differences. Cons: Interaction limited; for participants who are highly verbal; requires access to technology; costly.

Force field analysis Diagramming of a problem based on the assumption that any situation is a temporary balance between opposing forces. The driving forces facilitating change and those restraining change are identified and rated according to their importance by drawing arrows on the diagram *(see page 27)* to weight the strength of the force according to analyzer perception. Strategies for changing the most important resisting forces or strengthening facilitators are developed according to these goal-setting criteria: **S** -Specificity. Exactly what are you trying to accomplish? **P** -Performance. What behavior is implied? **I** -Involvement. Who is going to do it? **R** -Realism. Can it be done? **O** -Observability. Can others see the behavior? The acronym **SPIRO** can aid your thought process.

STRUCTURED GROUPS

Nominal Group Process Allows for idea generation and evaluation while avoiding the problems of group dynamics. Overcomes problem of a few individuals dominating the discussion. Requires room large enough for all participants, tables for 6-9, flip chart, and index cards. Takes 2-4 hours.

Steps: 1) Develop questions for participants requiring differentiated solutions; 2) Break-out groups should represent all perspectives in large group; 3) Participants answer questions by writing on cards, no discussion allowed; 4) Ideas are recorded on flip chart in round robin; 5) Explanation and clarification then encouraged but no criticism or collapsing; 6) Each group member privately ranks top ideas (e.g., top five); cards handed in and recorded on flip chart; 7) Brief clarifying discussion; 8) Private ranking again by each member and rankings from all subgroups combined for overall tally; 9) Cycle repeated for each question or issue.

Focus Group Process Small group discussion with structured and open-ended questions. Sampling is purposive, not random, to represent target population perspective. Similar to open-ended interviews but responses are not independent. However, allows for quicker data collection. If results are at variance with expectations based on other need identification techniques, additional data collection may be required. Useful for formative evaluation and program/materials development.

Delphi Panels A form of group process that generates a consensus through a series of questionnaires. Usually the respondents are unable to meet in one place due to geographical or time limitations. It is used as a forecasting technique and also to clarify, prioritize, or identify problems and solutions. Process involves three groups: decision makers, staff, and respondent group. Sometimes the decision makers and the staff are the same group. A questionnaire consisting of one or two broad questions is sent to the respondents. Their responses are analyzed and from these, a second questionnaire is developed. More specific questions for further clarification are included, their responses are again analyzed, and another questionnaire is sent out asking for additional information. The usual number of rounds is three to five.

Pros: Appropriate when precise information is not available; people separated by geography can be involved (often the experts); conformity, domination, or conflict is reduced since no face-to-face; written responses encourage quality and quantity; ideas given equal representation; usually highly committed individuals; feedback enables participants to respond throughout process and have a sense of closure at end.

Cons: Large amount of administrative time and cost; less opportunity to clarify meaning of specifics; no opportunity for dialogue and interaction; considerable time commitment for participants; less reward for respondents who must be highly committed.

INDIVIDUAL ASSESSMENT

Health Risk Appraisal/Assessment (HRA) Describes an individual's chance of becoming ill or dying from a particular cause over a period of time. Not a traditional medical appraisal for detection and identification of disease but a statement of probability. It is based on a comparison with mortality statistics and epidemiological data and is focused on behavior and personal characteristics. Demonstrates relationship between certain risk factors and specific causes of death or disability. It is intended to raise individual level of awareness/knowledge of personal risk factors and potential health outcomes; serve as a vehicle for health education counseling to promote voluntary health-related behavior change; serve as group needs assessment instrument for planning health education/health promotion programs. Often computerized. Privacy and confidentiality is a critical issue in worksite settings where this tool is usually used. It is useful also for adult health promotion programs in other settings.

Checklist Needs Assessment A list of topics that potential participants check to indicate interest. Easy to administer and tally and clients seldom object. Problem is that checklists usually reflect what professionals are ready to teach, not necessarily the interests of patients. Useful if carefully constructed. Leave space for "other," include topics from both patients and professionals, use focus group for construction.

For a comprehensive collection of HRA instruments, see Breckon, page 109. *(Breckon, 1994)*

STEPS IN DESIGNING AND COMPLETING A SURVEY *(Dever, 1991)*

1. Determine the objectives. Be sure to consult with those who have interests or outcomes at stake (the stakeholders).

2. Define the population groups to be studied.

3. Determine the specific data to be collected and the methods of measurement.

4. Choose the sampling unit and the sample size.

5. Determine the method of contacting individuals–interview, mailed questionnaire, telephone. Plan methods to reduce nonresponse rates.

6. Construct the questionnaire to obtain the desired information. Use existing validated items when possible. Field test.

7. Organize and carry out the interviews. Hire, train, and manage interviewers. Determine how refusals and nonresponses will be handled.

8. Process and analyze the data. This includes coding, keypunching, tabulating, and selecting appropriate statistical methods to specify relationships and significance.

9. Report the results. These should include implications and recommendations for actions.

II. PLANNING EFFECTIVE HEALTH EDUCATION PROGRAMS

1. *What is the most important component of a health promotion program aimed at lowering cholesterol?*
   a) *Measuring blood cholesterol levels of all participants, before, during and after program*
   b) *Educating participants about reducing fat consumption*
   c) *Demonstrating proper food selection and preparation*
   d) *Having a Registered Dietician on staff*

2. *If you were just starting a new health promotion program, with which group would you work?*
   a) *An established, local media health and medical journalist*
   b) *The local health officials*
   c) *A community-based organization*
   d) *A group of local doctors and nurses*

3. *What is the first step in a behavioral diagnosis?*
   a) *Identifying predisposing factors*
   b) *Listing enabling factors*
   c) *Identifying the barriers to change*
   d) *Selecting the health problem to be analyzed*

4. *Two major factors inherent in the Health Belief Model are:*
   a) *Beliefs about perceived seriousness and causal attribution*
   b) *Belief in susceptibility and belief in benefits of treatment*
   c) *Cues to action and dissonance reduction*
   d) *Adoption and maintenance of new behavior*

5. *Reciprocal determinism in Social Learning Theory posits:*
   a) *The continuing adaptation and change between the individual, the behavior, and the environment*
   b) *A stage of precontemplation before change*
   c) *The perception or belief in a person's ability to perform*
   d) *The occurrences independent of a person's action that makes the individual feel helpless*

6. *In the PRECEDE model, which of the factors in the educational diagnosis deals with the support functions of parents and/or health providers?*
   a) *Enabling*
   b) *Predisposing*
   c) *Reinforcing*
   d) *Communicating*

7. Within a target population, cultural differences initially should be considered during program:
   a) Planning
   b) Implementation
   c) Evaluation
   d) Marketing

8. At the completion of the program, 70% of the students in the School District will improve their physical fitness by 25%. This is:
   a) An outcome objective
   b) An impact objective
   c) A goal statement
   d) A process objective

9. Within five years of the initiation of the program, the adults in Mohawk County will attain the national average of 1.8 dental visits per year. This is:
   a) A behavioral objective
   b) A social marketing baseline measure
   c) A program objective
   d) An action and confirmation measure

10. In the process of selecting which educational method to use in a health education program, it is most important to:
    a) Ensure that only one method is selected for implementation
    b) Realize that all methods are equally useful in any setting
    c) Recognize that time and the program location rarely affect method selection
    d) Consider the nature of the audience and the purpose of the program

DEFINITION — "Planning is the process of establishing priorities, diagnosing causes of problems, and allocating resources to achieve objectives.

The implication of planning is that social problems are remedial in ways that are generally acceptable to those affected by them.

Planning and evaluation for health must take into account the entire fabric of society and its institutions — in essence, the community." *(Dever, 1991)*

The definitions, methods, and concepts of community organization can be applicable to a school, corporation, or medical-care setting as well as community. Additional definitions and concepts can be found in the community settings section.

"A community is a group of people with some things in common who are aware of those commonalities." *(Breckon, 1994)*

- *Collaborate with community agencies and individuals by coordinating resources and services.*
- *Collaborate with potential participants by involving them in plan development.*

A. COLLABORATE

Communicate a shared vision. Involve and mobilize target groups, significant others, resources. In school health programs, the collaboration is usually with parents. Analyze who has a positive and negative stake in change (stakeholders). Analyze power in an organization or community — location and degree.

Strategies for acceptance *(Craig, 1978)*

1. Explain the reason for changing.
2. Name the benefits that could result from the change.
3. Seek questions and answer them.
4. Invite participation.
5. Avoid surprise.
6. Acknowledge the rough spots.
7. Set standards (date for completion, what you want change to accomplish, identify penalties for failure, rewards for success).
8. Contact leaders.
9. Praise — give positive reinforcements.
10. Repeat — tell story over and over with fresh examples.

- *Develop the health education plan to meet health needs by applying theory and integrating assessment data, community resources and services, and input from potential participants.*

B. THEORY

The **PRECEDE** model is a useful framework for planning. *(Green, 1980)* It focuses on outcomes rather than starting with inputs, identifying specific educational steps to be completed in more detail than the Sullivan model. The steps are epidemiological and social diagnosis, behavioral diagnosis, educational and environmental diagnosis, and administrative diagnosis.

An additional step called **PROCEED** has been added to the administrative diagnosis in the newest edition of this model. *(Green & Kreuter, 1991)* This extends the consideration of **P**olicy, **R**egulatory and **O**rganizational barriers that could facilitate or hinder the development of the educational or environmental program during the implementation phase. Applying **PROCEED** at the behavioral and environmental diagnostic phase (Phase 3) or the **MATCH** model *(Simons-Morton, 1995)* while planning is also important to determine whether your target for the educational diagnosis should be (for example) policy makers, resource allocators, or parents rather than those who manifest the problem.

The **PRECEDE** model is also used to plan educational programs in organizational settings such as worksite, medical care, and schools. The organization's mission may impinge on the goals and objectives of your plan. *(See the Needs Assessment section, page 21, for additional comments about organizational analysis.)*

Organization development (OD) is the application of a long-range, planned-change technology to improve problem-solving and renewal processes by means of which an organization changes its culture. Two of the OD methods particularly useful for health educators are team building and conflict management. *(Ross, 1984)*

C. DEVELOP A PLAN

Plan for the plan. Analyze your own agency. *(See page 21 Needs Assessment)*
Logical scope and sequence.
Program planning is based on written plans that include the following elements: program goals, measurable objectives, appropriate activities, description of resources necessary, evaluation procedures. <u>Evaluation procedures are developed before program implementation and included in the written program plan.</u> *(Standards of Practice, 1991)*

In the effort to help program planners by reducing planning to a formula, a number of models have been proposed over the years. Simons-Morton notes that despite their important differences in sequence, emphasis, and conceptualization, the underlying principles that guide the models' development are similar. *(Simons-Morton, 1995)* Earlier models were **PERT** (**P**rogram **E**valuation and **R**eview **T**echnique), a timeline for specific milestones and outcomes *(see page 46)*; Sullivan's step model, and Mico's six-stage model. *(Mico, 1980)*

Subsequent more elaborate models incorporate similar steps or stages: initiation, needs assessment, goal setting.

PRECEDE — PROCEED is described in the previous section.

PATCH (**P**lanned **A**pproach **T**o **C**ommunity **H**ealth), which builds on the original **PRECEDE** model, is sponsored by the U.S. Public Health Service and provides resources to local communities and synergy with state and federal programs. Its goal is to increase the capacity of local communities to achieve the Year 2000 objectives. *(CDC)*

MATCH (**M**ultilevel **A**pproach **T**o **C**ommunity **H**ealth) focuses less on individual behavior change and more on organizational, community, and governmental levels. *(Simons-Morton, 1988)*

HEALTHY CITIES is a community organization model, sponsored by WHO, bringing all of the key

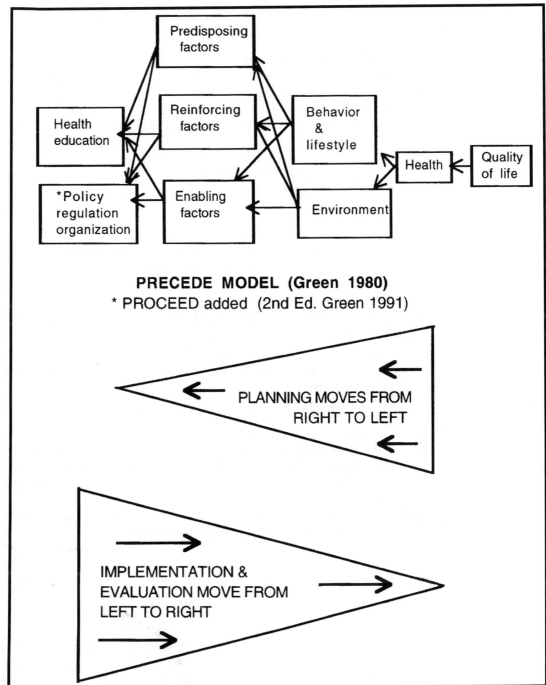

Figure 7
PRECEDE
MODEL

PRECEDE MODEL (Green 1980)
* PROCEED added (2nd Ed. Green 1991)

PLANNING MOVES FROM RIGHT TO LEFT

IMPLEMENTATION & EVALUATION MOVE FROM LEFT TO RIGHT

subsystems or sectors together with health as a primary focus. The goal is making individuals and communities healthy and whole. *(Duhl, 1996)*

HEALTHY PEOPLE 2000 is the most important planning tool and reference point for health program planners. It contains the health objectives for the U.S. each decade. The objectives are subsumed under 1) Health Promotion: physical activity, nutrition, tobacco, alcohol and other drugs, family planning, mental health, violent and abusive behavior, educational and community-based programs; 2) Health Protection: injury prevention, environmental health; 3) Preventive Services *(USDHHS, 1990)*

Two important reminders in planning:
Evaluation procedures must be developed before program implementation and included in your written plan.

Plan for the plan: Map the political terrain, find out who should be involved, assess scope, timing, cost of planning, and payoffs. The estimates of potential acceptance will guide you in estimating the scope and effort to invest.

D. FORMULATE APPROPRIATE AND MEASURABLE PROGRAM OBJECTIVES

Written objectives communicate to all other persons the direction and intent of the plan.
Checklist for objectives
- Objectives should be clear statements.
- Objectives should include just one indicator.
- Objectives should state reasonable time frames.
- Outcome objectives should be stated as performance, not effort.
- Objectives should be realistic and within the control of those responsible.
- Qualities of an objective: relevant, logical, unequivocal, feasible, observable, measurable.

Use the **PRECEDE MODEL** to carry out social diagnosis, epidemiological diagnosis, and behavioral diagnosis. Select a minimum of three strategies based on predisposing, reinforcing, and enabling factors, and use them to write your learning objectives. *(Green et al., 1980)*

LEVELS OF OBJECTIVES FOR COMMUNITY PLANNING

> **Goal or mission statement.** A broad, timeless statement of long-range program purpose. It should summarize the elements of the problem statement in positive outcomes and should include the health problem or issue to be changed and the target population. It is related to the epidemiological and social diagnosis in **PRECEDE**.

Author Comment

Warning! There is semantic confusion in this area. A number of people interchange the words "goals" and "objectives." These definitions are based on the agreement of the authors who are referenced under this section.

> **Program objectives.** Objectives are related to the goal but are specific, measurable statements of what you want to accomplish at a given time (usually 3-5 years). One or two usually cover your goals. They are **outcome** or future-oriented and related to health status. It is a specific statement of the health problem reflected in the social and epidemiological phases of **PRECEDE** and include the following elements: **WHO** will do **HOW MUCH** of **WHAT** by **WHEN?**

- Specify your target population in more detail

- Select target of intervention
    Influence governments for resources and policy changes
    Influence community or organizations for resources, policy and social norms changes; to reach influentials
    Influence gatekeepers/influentials to reach/train groups, provide reinforcement
    Influence individuals for behavior change or social support

- Identify several strategies to accomplish each objective: e.g., media, community organization, formal instruction, social support, training for providers, reinforcements, rewards

Author Comment

Note: Formal instruction is only one strategy and alone is not considered sufficient community education strategy. It may be viable for school classrooms or some workplace programs, for some patient education classes, or for training providers. It's difficult to get people to sit still. Think of all the ways that people get information and discuss and experiment with health issues in their daily lives in selecting several other interventions.

The use of focus groups as a formative evaluation measure is very useful at this juncture. The key to their value is the selection of participants and the types of questions that are posed. The technique provides target group perceptions and emotions in informal group discussions related to the issue. It provides you with useful clues about messages, types of interventions, and new viewpoints.

> **Impact objectives** describe the behaviors or actions that will resolve the problem and get you to your program goal (usually 1-3 years). They are also written as **WHO** will do **HOW MUCH** of **WHAT** by **WHEN?** In the **PRECEDE** model this phase is called the Behavioral Diagnosis.

Evaluation planning starts here while you are drafting program and impact objectives. Think about how you will tell when the change has taken place? What will people be doing that they aren't doing now?

What is the indicator or measure that you will use to measure your success? By adding this now, your evaluation steps are already evolving.

> **Add measurement criteria to your objectives** with a sentence specifying indicators. (How can you tell that there has been a change — how much change is needed to be acceptable?)

Identify the percentage of change (the number of participants or the amount of an observed action). Objectives should articulate those outcomes that must be accomplished to make the program worth the effort and expense. Think about:

How much change will make any noticeable difference?
How difficult will it be to effect change?
How much change has been reported in studies of similar programs?
How expensive or elaborate is the program?
What is the current level of the indicator to be changed?

> **Process or learning objectives** are the educational or learning tasks that must be accomplished to achieve the impact objectives of the intervention. They are based on the analysis of predisposing, reinforcing, and enabling factors in the **PRECEDE** model and are specified as knowledge changes, attitude and belief changes, behaviors and skills that are required of the target group or surrounding persons — parents, teachers, peers, providers, reporters, voters, etc. These make up the daily delivery of the educational activities and are subject to adjustment as they are tested. They are usually short-term but can have longer time spans depending upon the design of the program.

Table 2
LEVELS OF
OBJECTIVES
AND OUTPUTS

Objective	Outcome	Evaluation
A. GOAL	Ameliorate Health Problem	Changeability, Feasibility
B. PROGRAM OBJECTIVE	Outcome — Change in Morbidity, Mortality, Quality of Life	Health Change Attributable to Program?
C. ACTION/BEHAVIORAL OBJECTIVE	Impact — Behavioral Adaptation	Action or Desired Behavior? Attributable to Health Education Program?
D. PROCESS/LEARNING OBJECTIVES	Process — Change in Knowledge, Attitude, Practices	Measures of Change Knowledge, Habit, Attitude, Skill, etc… .
E. PROCESS/ ADMINISTRATIVE OBJECTIVES	Activities/Tasks on Schedule, Efficient	Exposure, Attendance, Materials, Schedules, Participation, etc… .

Process or administrative objectives are the daily tasks and work plans that lead to accomplishment of all of your planned objectives.

When you plan, move from the big idea down to the daily tasks — from the abstract to the concrete. When you implement you start at the opposite end with the daily concrete activities and move up to the more abstract, generalized objectives. Moving from the concrete to the bigger, more abstract concepts is also true of evaluation.

The questions that you ask at the process level after your start-up are: Is the program working? Are people coming to the event? Listening to the radio? If they are exposed, are they learning? Or if you are training, are the trainees displaying new skills? Do your clients understand the material? At the learning process level the question is: Are the methods we chose working? Can we detect changes in attitudes, skills, knowledge? Are we doing the best we can with our resources? Or should we change our methods and try to improve?

At the behavioral or impact level the evaluation question is one of efficacy. Can the action or behavior that will affect the health problem be detected? Can it be attributed to our program?

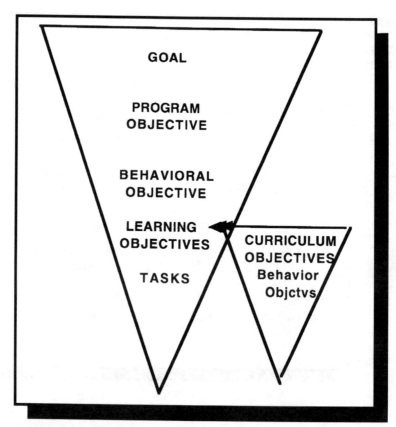

**Figure 8
RELATIONSHIP OF
INSTRUCTIONAL
BEHAVIORAL
OBJECTIVES TO
COMMUNITY HEALTH
PROGRAM
OBJECTIVES**

GOAL

PROGRAM
OBJECTIVE

BEHAVIORAL
OBJECTIVE

LEARNING
OBJECTIVES

TASKS

CURRICULUM
OBJECTIVES
Behavior
Objctvs

Curriculum Objectives and Goals in School Health

Goals are statements of broad intent that provide direction in making instructional decisions — long-range targets toward which instruction is directed. They are more general than objectives and are timeless. Objectives are short-term, precise statements of end results that build cumulatively toward a goal and in turn a topic or generalization. Effective complete objectives have a content dimension and a behavioral dimension. Precision in formulating and stating objectives can contribute to more effective teaching. The range of behaviors for learners in school health education curriculum should center around the general areas of information acquisition, skill development, concept development, opinion expression and development, and values awareness. *(Fodor, 1995)*

Note: Behavioral objectives in writing curriculum are considered an activity or process objective in community health education planning. Successful learning may result in observable behaviors but at this level seldom resolve health problems. Mager's historical book, which defined behavioral or measurable objectives, was describing curriculum objectives in programmed instruction. Don't confuse them with the behaviors sought at the impact level, which aim to reduce health problems.

E. DESIGN EDUCATIONAL PROGRAMS CONSISTENT WITH OBJECTIVES

The first questions to be asked in selecting strategies and designing an educational program for community health are: What specific behaviors must the learners acquire or enhance to reduce the effect of the problem? What information and skills must be gained for them to act in a new way or to maintain an existing way? What resources are needed? What related services or other kinds of conditions are required? Of all the desired changes, which actual actions can be addressed in the educational program?

Methods must be applied or activities must be performed to accomplish the short-term objectives. This program planning defines content, methods, time allotments, materials, facilitators, or instructors. A complete set of methods or process objectives constitute a work plan for the program. These activities are inputs that specify a time frame and a target group and they then refer to something the target group will receive or do.

These processes make up the objectives that are monitored, adjusted, or redesigned during the process evaluation stage. *(See Section III Implementation, page 43 for detail.)* Tasks are related to activities and refer to management or administrative tasks that the agency or personnel must do.

From the activities or tasks, personnel assignments, budgets, and time plans, personnel responsibilities evolve that must be recorded and monitored to manage the project.

"In school education the behaviors are cognitive and affective performance. Behaviors are focused on 'didn't know how to do, and now can do.' This is the acceptable level of behavior in curriculum objectives." *(Pollock, 1992)*

PRELIMINARY NOTES FOR THE PLANNER

Plan with people
Plan with data
Plan for permanence — staff time most expensive ingredient
Plan for priorities
Plan for outcomes and impact
Plan for evaluation
Plan for the plan
    Who should be involved
    Data needed
    Best time to plan
    Where it should occur
    Anticipate resistances
    What will enhance success of project
    Timetable *(Gantt or Pert Chart, see page 46)*

EVALUATION PLANNING IS PART OF PROGRAM DESIGN

After answering the questions that are noted at the beginning of Section 2.3, Designing Educational Programs, continue the raising of questions to articulate the evaluation issues: What actions or behaviors can and should you try to measure? What specific measures will be used and when? What educational techniques or methods are best and how can you monitor them? Do you need to plan training for agency staff or for program personnel? What organizational resources or arrangements are needed? What budget is required? Is your organization able and willing to provide the required resources?

Pre-implementation Checklist: *(Forouzesh, 1991)*

1. Clearly determine who does what, for whom, in what order, by when, and with what resources.

2. Develop and translate existing policies and procedures.

3. Assess required resources and their sources.

4. Determine and delegate administration and management responsibilities.

5. Develop an efficient communication network.

6. List all steps required and the order in which they must occur.

7. Determine when (date) each step should begin and end.

8. Identify internal and external constraints and factors that facilitate and support the implementation process such as policy-makers, parents, etc.

9. Make sure to monitor and reconfirm the commitment of all those involved in the process.

10. Design monitoring and tracking process to evaluate success of activities and need for adjustment or redesign if it isn't working. *(See Section IV Evaluating, page 51)*

11. Develop a contingency "what if" plan based on what can go wrong, will!

12. Identify implications and the impact of your program on other programs.

13. Identify the most crucial and important steps and activities to complete your program.

III. IMPLEMENTING HEALTH EDUCATION PROGRAMS

1. *Generally, which one of the following is the least expensive and most effective method of data collection in most circumstances?*
   a) *Random household survey*
   b) *Mailed, self-administered questionnaire*
   c) *Telephone survey*
   d) *Focus group interviews.*

2. *At the AIDS Task Force meeting, a business professional group member asks you a specific question about how the virus works in the body. You have recently read this information, but don't remember the details. Your most professional response is:*
   a) *Tell the person what you remember*
   b) *Tell the person that that subject will be covered at the next session*
   c) *Tell the person that their concern is not necessary.*
   d) *Say "I have some material on that question that I can mail to you."*

3. *You have invited representatives of several organizations to a meeting to talk about health needs in a neighborhood that has a series of divisive issues. You would like to avoid a conclusion that represents the narrow point of view of a few who speak loudly and may not reflect the whole community. As the responsible staff member, what is the best way to ensure that community-wide views are represented?*
   a) *Add additional representatives and increase participation*
   b) *Supplement the proceedings with a community survey*
   c) *Label the committee as an ad hoc task force group so that its existence can be limited*
   d) *Try to keep the group as small as possible*

4. *You anticipate divisive advocacy at the above meeting. For establishing issues or problems in priority order, the best meeting procedure is:*
   a) *Close the meeting to media representatives*
   b) *Apply parliamentary rules with a formal agenda*
   c) *Use nominal group process*
   d) *Divide into focus groups*

• *Implement the health education plan by employing health education methods and techniques to achieve program objectives.*

DEFINITION — Implementation is a systematic approach to putting decisions into the action phase or simply to put a designed plan into action.
   Criteria for implementation: (*Standards of Practice, 1991*)

Implementation is based on activities and timelines developed in a written plan; it is monitored for necessary adjustments; it includes close collaboration with community groups and leaders.

Before implementing, address the following issues: 1. Is this program acceptable to the target population? 2. Are there adequate resources available to ensure the continuation of the program? 3. Is this program legal and do you have the authority to deliver this program?

PROCESSES

1. Planning, conducting, attending meetings
    Purpose of meeting — representation of attendees
    Objectives — selection of format
    Roles — presider, discussion leader, participant
    Skills — summarize, keep discussion on track, encourage participation, know parliamentary procedure for formal discussion
2. Group dynamics
    Facilitate group cohesiveness, decision making, problem solving, shared leadership
    Facilitate cooperation and feedback
    Liaison between individuals or group and outside
    Assist in problem analysis and alternative solutions
    Assist in understanding of issues
3. Monitoring program activities
    Develop record system for feedback
    Revise activities based on process evaluation
4. Manage project or program
    Job descriptions, hire, supervise, evaluate personnel
    Monitor budget expenditures
    Develop time and task plan, objectives
    Regular reporting to executive board, funder, etc.
    Public relations and marketing strategies
    (See Section VII Communicating, page 67)
5. Build participation and trust with target groups and agencies

Table 3
EXAMPLE OF IMPLEMENTATION WORKSHEET FOR ACTIVITIES
Once you have identified the processes to be accomplished, use a worksheet to identify all of the daily tasks and timetables required to reach those objectives.
This sheet can be translated into a Gantt or PERT chart. See Figures 9 and 10, page 46.

RESOURCES:

Schedules, deadlines, etc...

Activities	Who Does What?	When?
1.		
2.		
3.		
4.		
5.		
6.		
etc... .		

Figure 9
TIME AND TASK PLAN OR GANTT CHART

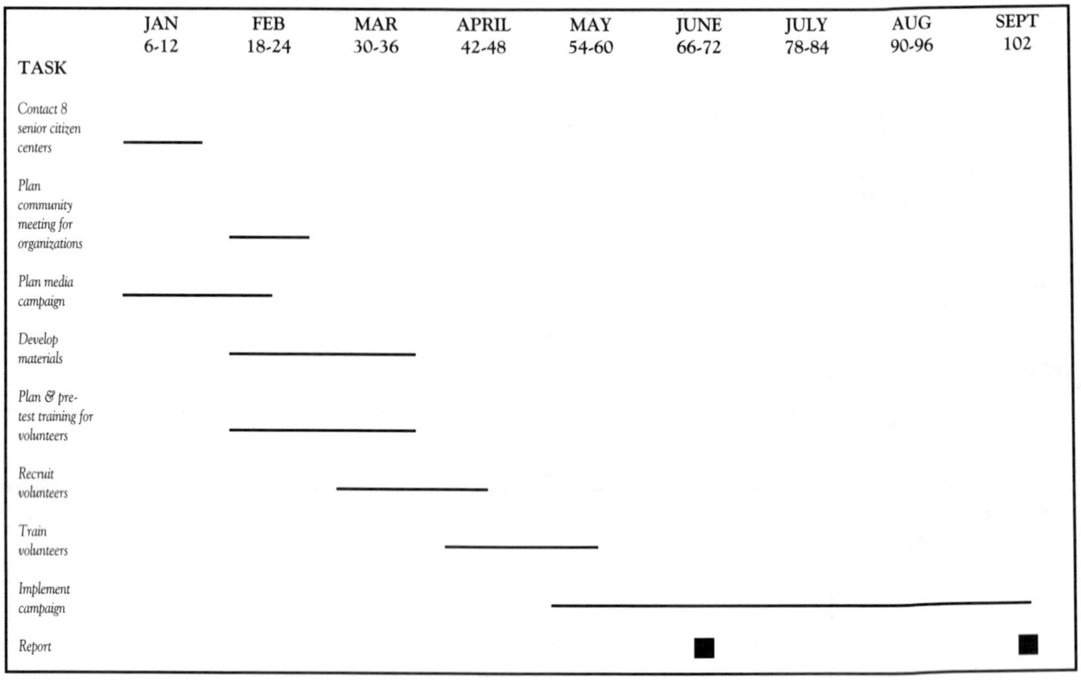

JAN 6-12
FEB 18-24
MAR 30-36
APRIL 42-48
MAY 54-60
JUNE 66-72
JULY 78-84
AUG 90-96
SEPT 102
TASK
Contact 8 senior citizen centers
Plan community meeting for organizations
Plan media campaign
Develop materials
Plan & pre-test training for volunteers
Recruit volunteers
Train volunteers
Implement campaign
Report

Figure 10
PROGRAM EVALUATION AND REVIEW TECHNIQUE (PERT)

Contact Senior Citizen Groups
Present Education Sessions
Schedule & Plan Meetings
90 days
PROJECT BEGINS
180 days
Media Campaign Plan
Schedule Media
SENIOR SAFETY CAMPAIGN IMPLEMENTED
Plan training
Contact Clubs
120 days
Train volunteers
Recruit volunteers

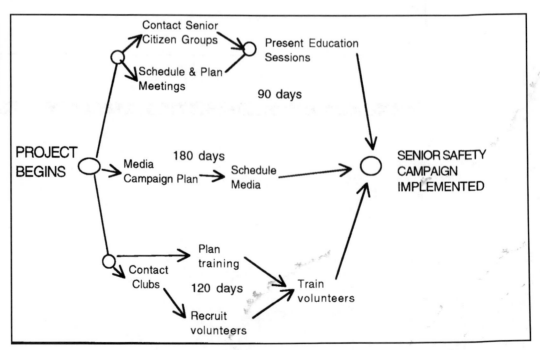

ETHICS

We have included the codes of ethics in this section because many of our encountered ethical dilemmas occur in the course of our daily work. These statements of our common values serve as guidance for general decision making in our professional and personal lives.

THE AMERICAN ASSOCIATION OF HEALTH EDUCATION

Adapted from **Code Of Ethics For Health Educators** *(AAHE, 1994)*

I. RESPONSIBILITY TO THE PUBLIC

Health Educators:
- Support the right of individuals to make informed decisions regarding their own health
- Encourage actions and social policies that support the balance of benefits over harm
- Accurately communicate the potential benefits and consequences of services
- Act on conditions that can adversely affect the health of individuals and communities
- Are truthful about their qualifications and the limitations of their expertise
- Are committed to providing professional services equitably to all people.

II. RESPONSIBILITY TO THE PROFESSION

Health Educators:
- Maintain their professional competence
- Treat all individuals equitably
- Encourage and accept critical discourse
- Contribute to the development of the profession by sharing program components they find to have been effective
- Do not manipulate or violate others' rights
- Are aware of possible conflicts of interest and exercise integrity
- Give appropriate recognition to students and colleagues for their professional contributions.

III. RESPONSIBILITY TO EMPLOYERS

Health Educators:
- Accurately represent their own qualifications and the qualifications of others
- Use current professional standards, theory, and guidelines as criteria when accepting consultation, delegating activities, and making referrals
- Accurately represent potential program outcomes to employers
- Make known competing commitments, conflicts of interest, and endorsements
- Openly communicate to employers when expectations or job assignments conflict with professional ethics.

IV. RESPONSIBILITY IN THE DELIVERY OF HEALTH EDUCATION

Health Educators:

- Are sensitive to a variety of cultural and social norms
- Promote the rights of individuals and groups to be actively involved in all aspects of process
- Use educational strategies and methods that reflect the Code of Ethics and applicable laws
- Implement strategies and methods that enable individuals through choice not coercion
- Conduct regular evaluations of program effectiveness
- Provide interventions that are grounded in theory and supported by empirical evidence.

V. RESPONSIBILITY IN RESEARCH AND EDUCATION

Health Educators:

- Conduct research in accordance with recognized scientific and ethical standards
- Ensure that consent of participants is voluntary and informed
- Implement standards to protect the rights, health, safety, and welfare of participants
- Maintain confidentiality and protect privacy of research participants
- Take credit, including authorship, only for work actually performed and give credit to others
- Serving as consultants, will discuss results only with those to whom they provide service, unless maintaining confidentiality would jeopardize others' health and safety.

Code Of Ethics (HEQ, 1994)

Health educators take on profound responsibility in using educational processes to promote health and influence human well-being. Ethical precepts that guide these processes must reflect the right of individuals and communities to make the decisions affecting their lives.

RESPONSIBILITIES TO SOCIETY

- To affirm an egalitarian ethic, believing that health is a basic human right for all
- To provide people with all relevant and accurate information and resources to make their choices freely and intelligently
- To support change by freedom of choice and self-determination, as long as these decisions pose no threat to the health of others
- To advocate for healthful change and legislation, and speak out on issues deleterious to the public health
- To be candid and truthful in dealings with the public, never misrepresenting or exaggerating the potential benefits of services or programs
- To avoid and take appropriate action against unethical practices and conflict of interest situations
- To respect the privacy, dignity, and culture of the individual and the community, and use skills consistent with these values.

RESPONSIBILITIES TO THE PROFESSION

- To share skills, experience, and visions with students and colleagues
- To observe principles of informed consent and confidentiality of individuals
- To maintain highest levels of competence through continued study, training, and research
- To further the art and science of health education through applied research and report findings honestly and without distortion
- To accurately represent capabilities, education, training and experience, and act within the boundaries of professional competence
- To ensure that no exclusionary practices be enacted against individuals on the basis of gender, marital status, age, social class, religion, sexual preference, or ethnic or cultural background.

IV. Evaluating Effectiveness Of Health Education Programs

1. Performance evaluation and review technique (PERT) is:
   a) An evaluation model
   b) A planning method suited to groups to set deadlines and schedules
   c) An indispensable management tool for small projects
   d) A list of all the tasks and personnel assignments

2. The best time to plan an evaluation is:
   a) When writing objectives for the overall program
   b) When beginning the implementation phase
   c) Just as soon as the implementation phase is underway
   d) Six (6) months before the program is completed

3. Cost-effectiveness is:
   a) The cheapest way to achieve the objective
   b) A measure of cost of intervention relative to its benefit
   c) The cost of intervention relative to its impact
   d) The intervention that has the most change

4. Asking participants in a blood pressure screening program to provide their reaction to the experience would be an example of:
   a) Formative evaluation
   b) Summative evaluation
   c) Criterion-referenced testing
   d) Monitoring process

5. In a project aimed at reducing heart attack, comparison of baseline blood pressure control levels to follow-up survey measures after a two-year intervention is completed is:
   a) A process evaluation
   b) An impact evaluation
   c) A formative evaluation
   d) An outcome evaluation

6. A determination that all members of a HMO should maintain blood pressure control measures of 140/90 or below is an example of:
   a) A criterion-referenced measure
   b) A norm-referenced measure
   c) A theoretical standard
   d) A summative evaluation

7. What type of evaluation is used to measure the effect(s) of the target group intervention?
   a) Summative
   b) Formative
   c) Process
   d) Critical

- Develop a program evaluation plan by establishing criteria of effectiveness to assess achievement of program objectives.
- Monitor the program by reviewing ongoing program activities to determine if the program is being implemented as planned.
- Monitor by comparing results with outcome criteria to determine program effectiveness.
- Modify the program as indicated by comparison of results with criteria to enhance the likelihood of program success.

A. EVALUATION PLANNING

See comments under the Planning section that refer to the relationship of program objectives to evaluation. See the attached table of relationships between **PRECEDE,** planning objectives, evaluation levels, and measurements. *(See page 53)*

- Evaluation is making a judgment based on comparison for the purposes of feedback to improve the quality of human services. Usual standards of comparison are historical (before and after); comparison with a group that has not had the intervention; or comparison with standards or norms from national data or theoretical outcomes from the literature.

- Difference between research and evaluation — research addresses issues of theoretical interest without regard for immediate concerns of organizations or people; evaluation generates information related to decision making and is done under time constraints. Research tools of varying degrees of rigor are used in evaluation.

- The purpose of evaluation is to answer one of two questions:

  a. "Are we doing the best we can with the resources that we have?" That is, are we using our resources efficiently — can we change our methods, materials, or program to be more effective? EFFICIENCY. This is process evaluation.

  b. "Is the program/intervention having any effect?" That is, are any changes that are observed the result of our program? This is called EFFICACY. This is impact evaluation.

c. There actually is a third question. The "So what?" question—did the program make any difference in health status? This is identified as the program goal. Changes in health are outcome evaluation. This is a longer-range question, requiring more resources and time and is usually not dealt with by entry-level health educators. However, it is important to keep the question in front of you as a compass.

**Figure 11
RELATIONSHIPS
BETWEEN PROGRAM
OBJECTIVES AND
EVALUATION LEVELS**

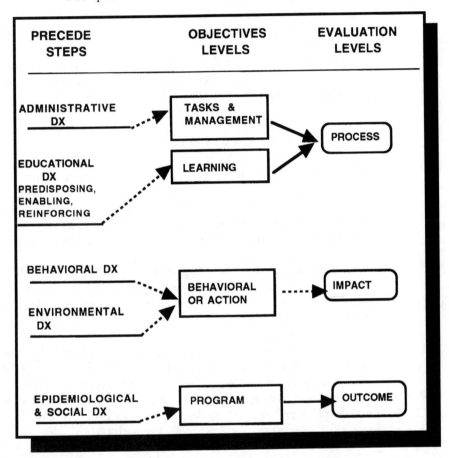

The three levels of evaluation objectives: link back to program objectives

a. Process — something changes as a result of planned learning and management activities

b. Impact — the intervention leads to an observable action/behavior that will have an impact on the health status

c. Outcomes — action/behavioral adaptation (b) leads to an improvement in health status

TYPES OF EVALUATION

Formative and **Summative** evaluation

These descriptors identify the **purpose or role** for the evaluation and do not refer to methods. Formative evaluation is ongoing improvement in an intervention, program or curriculum. It is done with the explicit purpose of early formation of data or making midstream alterations in the program to increase the likelihood of achieving the overall objective — in other words, to maximize the success of the intervention.

Summative evaluation assesses the extent to which a finished product or program causes changes in the desired direction in the target population and is justification for the expense of continuation in the present site and/or adoption in other settings. (*DeFriese, 1983*)

Qualitative vs. Quantitative evaluation

Qualitative evaluation data begin as descriptive information about programs and people in programs, whereas quantitative data can tell us whether change can be attributed to interventions and how much change there was in a program. Qualitative data can give us clues about why an intervention worked or did not work. For example, an observer might note that the relationship between the trainer and the trainees seems warmer with more interaction in one group than in a comparison group receiving similar skill training.

Qualitative methods produce large detail on smaller numbers of people and cases and are not constrained by predetermined categories. Quantitative data uses standardized measures that fit diverse responses into predetermined categories and can measure reactions of many to a limited set of questions. The latter facilitates comparison and statistical aggregation of data and provides a broad, generalizable set of findings.

Qualitative descriptions of processes are useful in understanding the dynamics of program operations: revealing areas in which programs can be improved, highlighting the strengths of the programs, permitting people not closely involved to understand how a program operates. They are useful for dissemination and replication of programs under conditions where a program has served as a demonstration project or is considered to be a model worthy of replication at other sites. Highly individualized programs that have individual goals such as tailored health promotion programs or counseling interventions may lend themselves to case descriptions. Validity and reliability are dependent upon trained, structured, consistent observations and reporting.

> Qualitative methods consist of three kinds of data collection:
> 1. in-depth interviews
> 2. direct observations
> 3. written documents (including questionnaires, personal diaries, program records)

The purposes and functions of these two methods are different but complementary. They are being used more together as multiple methods of evaluation have been encouraged. Subsequent comments are focused on quantitative evaluation.

Sources of Data for Evaluation

Records, agencies, census and vital statistics; program participants; staff delivering program; family members or significant others; reports, observations of evaluator; community-level indexes.

Evaluation Steps

Plan evaluation while program planning and before implementation.

    a. Choose the evaluation question, define purpose of evaluation — who wants to evaluate? Who are the stakeholders? Identify changes that can (should) be attributed to program.

    b. Select indicators for success of objectives *(See Section II Planning, page 31)*

        List levels of evaluation. *(Review Figure 11, page 53)*

        Plan evaluation steps.

    c. Evaluation design (purpose of the design is to eliminate systematic bias). What data need to be collected to answer what question? Select the comparison.

    d. Plan data collection: who, when, where, how, by whom, when.

    e. Identify or design measurement instruments.

    f. Select test statistics to determine degree and significance of changes detected.

Implementation

Management of evaluation — training of collectors, supervise, monitor

Data collection and reduction

- Analysis and interpretation of findings
- Reporting evaluation and advocating for change

The objective of the evaluation is to get the findings utilized by the decision maker and get the results incorporated into planning and implementation or to make modifications or recommendations.

Concepts

Cost benefit — A measure of the cost of an intervention relative to the benefits it yields, usually expressed as a ratio of dollars saved or gained for every dollar spent on the program.

Cost-effectiveness — A measure of the cost of an intervention relative to its impact, usually expressed in dollars per unit of effect. *(Green, 1986)*

Norm-referenced — Individual performance is compared to others in group (e.g., grading on the curve)

Criterion-referenced testing — Individual performance viewed as direct measure of content or skill assessed by test, with no reference to others.

Ethical standards —
>> Treatment of involved people
>> Role conflicts
>> Scientific quality of evaluation
>> Recognizing needs of all stakeholders
>> Negative effects
>>> Inaccurate findings can hurt people
>> Type I and Type II errors
>> Unplanned program effects

> **Validity and reliability of instruments** — Reliability is the extent to which the instrument will produce the same score if applied to an object two or more times.
> Validity is the extent to which the instrument measures what the evaluator wants it to measure or claims that it measures.

B. EVALUATION DESIGNS

Concepts

Sampling — A process by which a portion of the population is selected. The goal is to represent the population as closely as possible and minimize bias due to selection.

Probability Sample — A sample in which all elements of the population in a universe have a known probability of being selected. Probability samples are important because it is the only type of sample that allows the evaluator to treat the sample as technically representative of the larger population. Examples: simple random, stratified random, cluster samples.

Nonprobability Samples — Samples which are not representative of the population. Examples: convenience samples, homogeneous and heterogeneous samples.

Variable — name for an object of interest that is thought to influence (or be influenced by) something else. Independent (cause), dependent (effect) variables.

Language of design — 0 = observation, X = intervention or experiment, R = randomization. Designs are intended to measure change and determine if change is a result of the intervention. Things that can get in the way of the latter are called threats to validity (what can distort the outcome). These threats include: history, maturation, instrumentation, testing, selection, Hawthorne effect and attrition.

> a. Nonexperimental approaches (single-group designs) can assess usefulness of further evaluation; correlate improvements with other variables; prepare facility for further evaluation.
> These designs answer: How well are the participants functioning at the end of the program? Are minimum standards of outcome achieved? How much do participants change during their participation in the program? **They will not tell you that change was the result of the intervention/program.**

```
+-----------------------------------------------------------------------+
|          Single-group Designs/ Nonexperimental Examples               |
|                                                                       |
|   One observation              X 0                                    |
|                                                                       |
|   Two observations             01 X 02 ( also called pre/post-test)   |
|                                                                       |
|   Time Series                  0 0 0 0 X 0 0 0 0                       |
+-----------------------------------------------------------------------+
```

b. Quasi-experimental designs help evaluators identify if changes in program participants were the result of the program. This is done through 1) observing participants at additional times before and after the program, 2) observing additional people who have not received the program, and 3) using a variety of variables, some expected to be influenced by the program and others not expected to be affected. Particular health education concerns are biases caused by self-selection into the program; general community or societal changes, and the reactive effects of making observations.

```
+-----------------------------------------------------------------------+
|                Quasi-experimental Design Examples                     |
|                                                                       |
|   Non-equivalent                                                      |
|   Comparison group design                  0   X   0                  |
|                                             0       0                  |
+-----------------------------------------------------------------------+
```

The five elements of true experimental design are: 1) representative sample of target population; 2) one or more pretests; 3) unexposed group for comparison; 4) random assignment of the samples; 5) one or more post-tests to measure effects after the experimental intervention. (*Green and Lewis, 1986*)

True experimental or research design requires random assignment to control for bias and having all the elements that are listed above as the elements of research/evaluation design.

```
+-----------------------------------------------------------------------+
|                  Experimental Design Examples                         |
|                                                                       |
|   Experimental Group               (R) 0   X   0                      |
|                                                                       |
|   Control Group                    (R) 0       0                      |
+-----------------------------------------------------------------------+
```

C. DATA ANALYSIS

Statistics in education have these purposes:

   a. Summarize information such as measures of central tendency and measures of dispersion or variability.

b. Determine how seriously to regard differences observed: are they real or chance occurrences?

c. Determine the amount of relationship between data sets: correlation (correlation has an advantage over percentages because it allows you to capture in a single statistic both the direction and amount of association).

Four levels of measurement are:

a. Nominal — variables have labels but no numerical meaning
Example: red apples, yellow apples, green apples

b. Ordinal — implies levels of intensity or severity. One category is more or less than another. Categories are in sequence.
Example: sour apples, tart apples, sweet apples

c. Interval — variables have a standard unit of measure; e.g., miles, standardized test scores, degrees Fahrenheit

d. Ratio — standard unit of measure with an absolute zero; e.g., dollars, inches, degrees Centigrade

Measures of Central Tendency — The most frequently occurring category or mode is useful for describing the distribution of nominal data. The median is applicable to ordinal level data. The mean (the arithmetic average) is applicable to interval data except where you have extremes or outliers; the median (middle-most observation) is then used.

Three types of statistics:

a. univariate — distribution, measures of central tendency and dispersion, tests of significance

b. bivariate — measures of association — how strong

c. multivariate — measures of association, tests of significance, variance- measures of dispersion

Figure 12 NORMAL DISTRIBUTION OR BELL CURVE — THE BASIS FOR TESTS OF SIGNIFICANCE, as well as test grading procedures

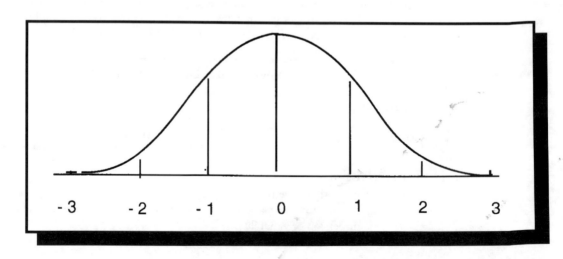

V. COORDINATING PROVISION OF HEALTH EDUCATION SERVICES

1. Saying "Let the boss or an impartial expert decide" is an example of conflict resolution by:
 a) Compromise
 b) Problem solving
 c) Fight or confrontation
 d) Flight or avoidance

2. Essentially, coalition building is based on:
 a) An organization's vested interests
 b) Collaboration
 c) Representativeness
 d) Equity in sharing resources

• *Elicit the cooperation of persons from diverse programs by establishing relationships with and between those individuals to coordinate related health education services.*

Two major approaches concerning interaction between organizations can be identified: collaboration and negotiation.

A collaborative approach requires organizations to identify unity and agreement between diverse groups and to harmonize ways of working together. A negotiating approach usually is based on different organizations pursuing their own interests. Collaboration is the basis for coalition building and important early in the planning process. It is based on politics, power, and resource allocation.

Conflict management is an important skill in gaining intergroup and intragroup cooperation and collaboration. Conflict to some degree always exists; it is a part of life. Therefore the goal is to manage conflict in constructive ways. There are three modes of management: 1) confrontation/fight includes win-lose power struggles, scapegoating, and third-party judgment; 2) collaborative confrontation includes problem solving, compromise, and peaceful coexistence; 3) avoidance includes withdrawal, isolation, indifference, and feigned ignorance.

Collaborative problem solving and compromise using negotiation is the most effective strategy. Steps in negotiation: 1) meet on neutral ground; 2) actively listen to each other; 3) assert self responsibly; 4) lower defenses; 5) seek consensus; 6) exercise a spirit of compromise; 7) seek satisfaction on both sides.

It is important to consider the makeup of the organizations when attempting to build collaborative and cooperative relationships.

Human service and health organizations have three levels or domains: policy, management, and service. Each approaches problems of service integration differently. Each has its own unique perspective and each tends to be in conflict with one or both of the other two domains. Medical centers are structured with three different social systems (board, management, service) as opposed to

one in industry. The systems lead to separate identifiers, interpretations of events, contrasting norms, discordance, struggle for control, different change rhythms, and uncertainty. *(Mico, 1980)*
Building interdisciplinary groups or teams as well as interagency collaboration requires dealing with issues such as goal setting, role expectation, negotiation, decision making, problem solving, leadership, and conflict management.

Health educators must develop plans for coordination, facilitate cooperation between various levels of program personnel and organizations, serve as liaison between groups, employ conflict reduction, and organize in-service training.

1. Networking — inducing change — power or resource base

    Identify supportive organizational or community relationships that benefit program(s)

    Promote cooperation and feedback

2. Conflict resolution and negotiation skills

3. In-service training

    Functions: identification of effective and efficient strategies and training methods, training of trainers, information and resource gathering, design of training modules, consultation on training methods, identification of and consulting with experts, coordinating training activities, evaluation design, and implementation of training. *(Standards of Practice, 1991)*

    a. How People Learn

        From reading and participating; with emotional impact and in the absence of threat; with illustration, with room for insight; with a framework, to satisfy adult needs, with a sense of responsibility and relevance; in a comfortable setting and with humor.

    b. Designing Training

        Needs assessment, objectives, use of time and space, preparation, evaluation.

    c. Training Methods

        Lecture, large group discussion, small group discussion, audiovisual use, role plays, exercises, and games.

        (See also Breckon for more comments on training.)

4. Team building

VI. ACTING AS A RESOURCE PERSON IN HEALTH EDUCATION

1. Which one of the following organizations asserts a primary responsibility for promoting international health?
   a) WHO
   b) UNICEF
   c) UNDP
   d) International Red Cross

2. Which one of the following is a voluntary agency?
   a) American Dietetic Association
   b) American Medical Association
   c) American Hospital Association
   d) American Cancer Society

3. You have been assigned to write a grant proposal on the prevention of violent and abusive behavior. Which one is the most appropriate database for initiating your search?
   a) Psychlit
   b) ERIC
   c) Medline
   d) Medlars

4. If you conduct a database search for information on harmful levels of certain chemicals in ocean fish consumed in Florida, what combination of key words would provide the best access to the information you need?
   a) Florida, fish, ocean, eating
   b) Fish, chemicals, Florida, consumption
   c) Ocean, fish, Florida, chemicals
   d) Morbidity, fishing industry, consumption, Florida

- Select sources of information on health issues by evaluating these sources to disseminate health information

Organize and keep up to date: directory of community health information resources; catalog of educational materials; current reference file of resources for health services and community information; a method to access this information by staff and public.

Expand resources: collaborate, recruit volunteers, seek contributions.

A. UTILIZE HEALTH INFORMATION RETRIEVAL SYSTEMS

Examples of health information databases that can be accessed through library sources are ERIC, PsychLit, and Medline. Librarians are helpful sources of information about how to use key words and zero in on special topics, but in this information age, health educators, like all other professionals, should be able to use electronic access for personal availability. Following are examples of health information resources available through phone, fax, and computer.

National Health Information Center, P.O. Box 1133, Washington, D.C. 20013-1133. Toll-free information numbers, and over 1100 health information resources. Write for the latest lists for your files.

CDP File (Chronic Disease Prevention File), a CD-ROM database, has seven databases of information about health promotion and disease prevention. Subjects are Health Promotion and Education, Comprehensive School Health, Cancer Prevention and Control, Prenatal Smoking Cessation, Epilepsy Education and Prevention, Smoking and Health, and Chronic Disease Prevention. Produced by the CDC, it is available from GPO, Washington D.C.

CHID, a computerized bibliographic database, is a unique reference service for health and education professionals who need to locate health information for themselves or their clients. Over 21 subfiles with more than 70,000 abstracted items are available on major health topics. For information and costs, call 1-800-289-4277.

GRATEFUL MED is a user-friendly software package for searching a variety of National Library of Medicine databases. For information, call National Network of Libraries of Medicine, 1-800-338-7657.

Especially for Health Educators:

HEEF The Health Education Electronic Forum, available by modem through a TCP/IP connection on the Internet, using First Class Client 2.6 software at 206.218.187.2 or heef.doe.state.la.us. There is room for files and conferences by your group or interest area. Free access to live on-line conferences. HEEF holds over 100 health education and health-related shareware and public domain software applications for PC and MAC. For more information, contact Michael Pejsach, fax 504-342-3354.

HEDIR The International Health Education E-mail Directory, a directory of health educators throughout the world and an electronic communications system for news of interest to professionals and students in the field of health education (listserv). For more information, e-mail Mark J. Kittleson (GA3748@SIUCVMB.SIU.EDU).

SELECT INTERNET RESOURCES FOR HEALTH EDUCATION

Sponsoring Agency	Internet URL
Gateway to Consumer Health and Human Services Information Website from the U.S. Government	http://www.healthfinder.gov
U.S. Dept. of Health and Human Services	http://www.os.dhhs.gov
U.S. Dept. of Education	http://www.ed.gov/
Natl. Health Info. Center, ODPHP Public Health Service	http://nhic-nt.health.org
Centers for Disease Control and Prevention	http://www.cdc.gov
National Institutes of Health	http://www.nih.gov
Virtual Public Health Center	http://www-sci.lib.uci.edu/ -martindale/PHealth.html
Distance Learning on the Net	http://www.interaccess. com/users/ghoyle/
Instructional Technology Connections	gopher://eenued.eudenver. edu/hO/ UCD/dept/edu/IT/ ryder/itcon.html
Global Campus	http://www.csulb.edu/ge/
American Public Health Association	http://www.apha.org
Health Education Resources on the Internet	http://www.personal.umich.on edu/jltuckerlhlth_603.html

INTERNET

The Internet is constantly growing and changing, so none of the information below is guaranteed. Listed are a few of the sources on the Web that are helpful to health educators. The search engines and catalogues are also changing and improving, but remember that none of them are comprehensive. Each works differently, so use a variety of tools.

"Search engines" (software to access the World-Wide Web) to try:
Alta Vista, Excite, Infoseek Guide, Lycos, NlightN, Open Text Index, Yahoo.

B. INTERPRET AND RESPOND TO HEALTH INFORMATION REQUESTS

Regardless of what information retrieval system you use, the steps in a literature search are the same: identify the need, match needs to likely sources, pursue leads, judge the quality and quantity, and organize the materials in the form most useful to the user in terms of categories, cross-references, and catalogue lists.

Don't overlook local, state, and professional organizations, newsletters, and reports as sources of information. These data are seldom found on the Internet or the national databases listed and are often germane to the issue at hand.

C. SELECT EFFECTIVE MATERIALS FOR DISSEMINATION

Use of instructional media —purpose, selection, standards, resources.

Criterion: Health information materials must have planned use; relate to interested audience, potential consumers, or special population groups in terms of age, culture, language, education, and literacy levels; incorporate principles of good publication design; be technically accurate; be pretested for accuracy, appropriateness, and effectiveness; be actively used and distributed; be kept current. (*Standards of Practice, 1991*)

Know and apply community standards — accuracy, community customs, and acceptability.

Fodor and Dalis (1995) criteria checklist: Contain a core of accurate information; at appropriate maturity level; economical in terms of time expended; readily available; expose clients to a variety of information; enable clients to acquire information at their own pace.

Breckon (1994) on effective development of materials: Printed materials should be attractive, interesting, uncluttered, readable, concise, important, timely, clear, motivating, and accurate.

Pretesting — 1) Planning and strategy selection; 2) Concept development; 3) Message execution.

Readability — Using a formula to predict the approximate grade level a person must have achieved to understand written material. It is based on the number of polysyllabic words and the length of the sentence. There are a number of readability formulas known by acronyms such as SMOG and FOG.

Framework Requirement

- *Serve as consultant by assisting in the identification of issues and recommending alternative strategies.*

D. CONSULTATIVE RELATIONSHIPS

- **Consultation — Purpose:** establish a helping relationship.
- **Definition:** A consultant is a person who is trying to have some influence over a group or organization but has no direct power to make changes or implement programs. *(Block)* Consultation is a two-way interaction — a process of seeking, giving, and receiving help. *(Lippett and Lippett, 1978)*
- **Cardinal condition:** Help is never really help unless and until it is perceived as helpful by the recipient, regardless of the helper's good intentions.
- Consultation is a conceptual tool for change agent role for individual, interpersonal, organizational, or interorganization change (other change agent tools are training and research). It is different from other roles such as training, supervision, administration, or counseling.
- Characteristics of the relationship: permissive, voluntary, temporary, supportive, disciplined, interactive — two-way process, and initiated by the consultee.
- Two components: technical expertise and an emotional component.
- Models — expert, pair of hands, collaborator, or problem solver.
- Six phases of consultation
    1. Contact and entry
    2. Contract and establish relationship
    3. Problem identification — analysis
    4. Goal setting and planning
    5. Taking action and cycling feedback
    6. Contract completion — design continuity and termination

VII. COMMUNICATING HEALTH AND EDUCATION NEEDS, CONCERNS, AND RESOURCES

1. A SMOG test measures:
    a) Impact of a visual image
    b) Reading level
    c) Scope of information in a document
    d) Environmental air quality

2. Which one of the following is the most appropriate statement when communicating health concerns?
    a) Fear messages in health education are never used because they are ineffective
    b) Fear messages are effective if they include an action that will reduce the fear
    c) Fear messages are effective in moderation
    d) Fear messages are unpopular

3. Most health educators continuously employ this technique to change behavior:
    a) Persuasive communication
    b) Advocacy skills
    c) Ethical conduct
    d) Group dynamics

4. To help promote behavioral change in a specific homogenous population, the best strategy is to approach the:
    a) Grass roots, general population
    b) Legislative power brokers in the community
    c) Target group
    d) Community leaders

Framework Requirement

- Keep abreast of professional literature, current trends, and research.
- Advocate for inclusion of education in health programs and services
- Explain the foundations of the discipline of health education, including its purposes, theories, history, ethics, and contributions, to promote the development and practice of health education.

The skill requirements that were used to set the general context for the field in the introduction are restated here, because they can also be applied to individual workers and to specific health education activities. The subject matter of health education to be interpreted is derived from the biological and behavioral sciences. The goal of health education centers around the promotion of wellness. Health educators must know how to apply learning and social change theories in relation to health and select and apply theories and concepts, programs, and activities.

Professional values must be clear. Health educators must be alert to discrimination, sensitive to the differences between education and manipulation, and able to employ a range of strategies for dealing with controversial health issues.

- *Select communication methods and techniques by matching the characteristics of individual target groups with methods/techniques and issues to assess, plan, implement, and evaluate health education services.*

SUMMARIES OF SELECTED HEALTH EDUCATION THEORIES AND MODELS

Adoption and Diffusion Theory *(Rogers, 1993)*—A process by which new products or ideas are introduced or "diffused" to the audience. The message will be accepted (or behavior adopted) based on whether the audience perceives it as beneficial, as in accordance with their needs and values, finds it easy or difficult to understand or adopt, can try the behavior, and feels that results of the trial are viewed positively by their peers. People adopt new ideas and changes at different rates. The socio-economic characteristics of groups and their rate of adoption have been classified into innovators, early adopters, early majority, late majority, and late adopters or hard to reach. The time that it takes for this process is called diffusion and can be taken into account when choosing strategies and interventions. *(See adoption curve under Community Settings.)* *(See readings for examples: Green et al.: Macro-Intervention to Support Health Behavior; Deeds and Gunitalake: Behavioral Change Strategies.)*

Behavioral Intention *(Fishbein, 1975)*—The likelihood of the target audience adopting a desired behavior can be predicted by assessing (and subsequently trying to change or influence) their attitudes toward and perceptions of the benefits of the behavior, along with how they think that their peers will view their behavior. An individual's and society's perceived attitudes are an important predecessor to action.

Behavioral Medicine *(Pomerleau, 1979)*—Clinical use of techniques derived from behavior therapy and behavior modification for the evaluation, prevention, management, or treatment of physical disease or physiological dysfunction. Concepts are behavioral epidemiology, learning and conditioning, biofeedback, and self-management.

Behaviorism *(Skinner, 1974)*—Concentrates on external, observable conditions in which behavior takes place. Behavior change is a response to environment. By administering positive or negative reinforcers (stimuli), patterns of behavior can be established or learned (response). Respondent or operant conditioning is directed toward manipulation of stimuli to evoke reflex behavior. It involves no intervening mental process or use of reinforcement schedules.

Cognitive Development Theory *(Piaget)*—Four major stages of cognitive development are described, each characterized by qualitatively different schemes and all experienced in order: 1) the sensory-motor stage (birth to age 2); 2) preoperational stage (age 2-7); 3) concrete operational stage (age 7-11); 4) formal operational stage (age 11 to adulthood). Preoperational children confuse cause and effects of illness and conceive of health and illness as two separate happenings, not ends of the continuum. They lack ability to generalize between similar experiences; they reason egocentrically. At the concrete operational stage, children tend to see health as ability to perform desired activities. They begin to grasp concept of causal sequencing and gradually become future-oriented. At the formal operational stage, children understand linkages between behavior and health outcomes and recognize individual susceptibility in onset of disease. This theory has implications for designing successful school health education.

Cognitive Dissonance (*Festinger, 1962*)—The simultaneous existence within a person of knowledge and beliefs that do not fit together (dissonance) leads the person to take efforts to make them fit better (dissonance reduction). Dissonance can arise as a consequence of decisions, temptation, group interactions, disagreement with others, forced public compliance, etc. Dissonance can be reduced by obtaining support from people who already believe or by persuading others that they too should believe what the person wants to persuade himself is true.

Coping Theory (*Folkman and Lazarus*)—Defined as "the person's constantly changing cognitive and behavioral efforts to manage specific external and/or internal demands that are appraised as taking or exceeding the person's resources." This theory takes in personal and situational factors. There are eight distinct ways of coping: confronting, distancing, self-control, seeking social support, accepting responsibility, escape-avoidance, problem solving, and positive reappraisal.

Field Theory (*Lewin, 1951*)—Human behavior is in a constant state of dynamic equilibrium, a quasi-stationary equilibrium caused by two sets of forces working against each other within the individual or the situation: forces toward behavior change and those resisting the movement. For every action there is a reaction. (*See force-field analysis under Assessment Tools for practical application of this theory.*)

Freezing-Unfreezing Theory (*Lewin, 1951*)—a) Unfreezing is a state of readiness-for-change in basic attitudes, motivations, and behaviors. b) Problem-diagnosis phase — identification of forces for and against change, and analysis of those forces in terms of how and where changes can be introduced. c) Goal-setting phase — establish specific goals and direction. d) Person experiments with range of new behaviors possible and practices those found to be the more desirable. e) Refreezing — newer learnings and changes found to be beneficial are assimilated into a more permanent framework of behavior. (*See Stages of Change Theory, page 71.*)

Health Belief Model (*Becker, 1987*)—Beliefs about perceived seriousness, susceptibility, benefits, and barriers affect person's health behavior. Each has a cognitive element — what might happen — and an affective component — how deeply one cares about the consequences. Cues that mobilize beliefs is a second component.

Learned Helplessness *(Seligman and Maier, 1967)*—When an event occurs independently of your actions, it can be the basic cause of learned helplessness. Three causal attributions are suggested: 1) internal vs. external — personal internal factors vs. external fate or bad luck; 2) global vs. specific — attribute failure to wide range of situations vs. being unsuccessful with specific factor; 3) stable vs. unstable — learned helplessness occurring occasionally or consistently over time. This suggests that intervention needs to emphasize cognitive and emotional as well as behavioral ways of handling uncertainty.

Persuasion in Communications *(McGuire, 1981)*—Individuals pass through a series of steps to assimilate a desired behavior: exposure to the message; attention to the message; interest in or personal relevance of the message; understanding; personalizing behavior to fit life; accepting change; remembering the message and continuing to agree with it; being able to think of it; making decisions based on bringing the message to mind; behaving as decided; receiving (positive) reinforcement for behavior; accepting the behavior into one's life.

To communicate the message successfully, five communication components all must work: the credibility of the message source; the message design; the delivery channel; the target audience; and the targeted behavior.

SMCR THEORY *(Berlon 1960)*—

**Figure 13
SMCR (SOURCE, MESSAGE, CHANNEL, RECEIVER) COMMUNICATIONS MODEL**
(Berlo 1960)

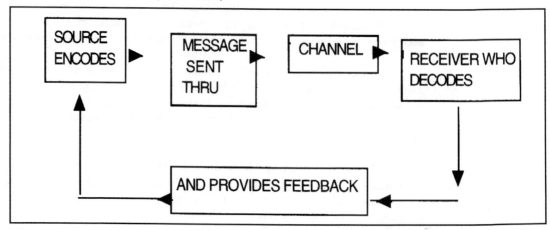

CHARACTERISTICS OF SOURCE — credibility, likeability, similarity
CHARACTERISTICS OF MESSAGE — order (first or last); one-side or two; fear; visuals; amount of evidence
CHARACTERISTICS OF CHANNEL — one medium vs. other, combinations, keep message simple, noise or distraction
CHARACTERISTICS OF RECEIVER — personality variables (self-esteem efficacy, anxiety, ego-defensiveness), ego-involvement (emotional commitment)

PRECEDE *(Green, 1980)*—A planning model with four steps: a social diagnosis, epidemiological diagnosis, behavioral and environmental diagnosis, and an educational and organizational diagnosis. In the educational and organizational diagnosis phase, involving predisposing, enabling, and reinforcing factors (from which the PRECEDE acronym is derived), a thorough behavior change analysis is carried out. A fifth step — policy, regulatory, and organizational analysis (PROCEED)— provides the environmental, resource, and political diagnosis required for change.

Self-Efficacy Theory *(Bandura, 1986)*—Perceived self-efficacy is defined as people's judgment of their capabilities to organize and execute courses of action required to attain designated types of performance. It is concerned not with the skills one has but with judgments or beliefs of what one can do with whatever skills one possesses. It is behavior-specific. You can have high efficacy for one behavior and low for another. It deals with our perception or belief that we can accomplish some future behavior — in this way it is predictive.

We can change self-efficacy: by skills mastery — a good way to accomplish mastery is to have clients contract for specific behaviors and give feedback; modeling — see someone else performing or coping or let group members solve problems; reinterpretation of physiological signs and symptoms — identify beliefs and reinterpret them; persuasion — urge toward short-term realistic goals and enlist high- credibility persuaders.

Social Learning Theory *(Bandura, 1986)*—(a.k.a. Social Cognitive Theory) Sharp contrast to behaviorism and is integrative, focusing on cognitive theories that emphasize internal factors such as attitudes, values, beliefs (we learn how to behave from our social interactions), and external determinants of behavior. Major concepts include environment, situation (person's perception), behavioral capability, expectation, expectancies, self-control, observational learning, reinforcements, self-efficacy, emotional coping responses, and reciprocal determinism (the dynamic interaction of person, behavior, and environment).

Stages of Change *(DiClemente, 1985)*—Assumption that chronic behavior does not change all at once, but on a continuum: 1) precontemplation— no interest, not thinking about change; 2) contemplation— serious thought given to change; 3) action— 6-month period after overt action taken; 4) maintenance— from 6 months to whenever behavioral problem is terminated (either by new habit or relapse).

MAJOR JOURNALS FOR HEALTH EDUCATORS

AWHP WORKSITE HEALTH
60 Revere Drive, Suite 500
Northbrook, IL 60062

AMERICAN JOURNAL OF HEALTH BEHAVIOR
PNG Publications
P.O. Box 4593
Star City, WV 26504-4593
(304) 293-4699

AMERICAN JOURNAL OF HEALTH PROMOTION
Allen Marketing & Management
P.O. Box 1897
Lawrence, KS 66044

AMERICAN JOURNAL OF HEALTH STUDIES
P.O. Box 870312
The University of Alabama
Tuscaloosa, AL 35487-0312
1-800-285-5293

AMERICAN JOURNAL OF PREVENTIVE MEDICINE
American College of Preventive Medicine
Elsevier Science Limited
Oxford, England
Phone: Country Code 44 1865 843-000

AMERICAN JOURNAL OF PUBLIC HEALTH
The American Public Health Association
1015 15th Street, N.W., Third Floor
Washington, D.C. 20005
(202) 789-5600

HEALTH EDUCATION AND BEHAVIOR
Society for Public Health Education
1015 15th Street, Suite 410
Washington, D.C. 20005
(202) 408-9804

HEALTH PROMOTION & EDUCATION
International Union for Health Promotion & Education
c/o Institut Sante et Developpement
15-21, rue de l'Ecole de Medecine
Phone: F-75270 Paris Cedex 06 France

HEALTH EDUCATION RESEARCH: THEORY & PRACTICE
Oxford University Press
2001 Evans Road
Cary, NC 27513
(919) 677-0977

INTERNATIONAL QUARTERLY OF COMMUNITY HEALTH EDUCATION
Baywood Publishing Co.
26 Austin Avenue
P.O. Box 337
Amityville, NY 11701

JOURNAL OF HEALTH EDUCATION
American Association for Health Education
1900 Association Drive
Reston, VA 20191
(703) 476-3437

JOURNAL OF SCHOOL HEALTH
American School Health Association
P.O. Box 708
Kent, OH 44240
(330) 678-1601

PATIENT EDUCATION & COUNSELING
Elsevier Science Publications
655 Avenue of the Americas
New York, NY 10010
(212) 989-5800

HEALTH EDUCATION PROFESSIONAL ORGANIZATIONS

American Association for Health Education (AAHE) [1]

The Association for the Advancement of Health Education is part of the larger American Alliance for Health, Physical Education, Recreation, and Dance, which comprises more than 43,000 professionals in sports, dance, safety education, physical education, recreation, and health education. AAHE has a membership of more than 7,500 professionals from schools, universities, community health agencies, and voluntary agencies. It promotes comprehensive health education programming in schools, colleges, and community settings. AAHE has a full-time staff that maintains close contact with legislative issues in Washington, D.C. For further information contact AAHE, 1900 Association Drive, Reston, VA 20191, (703) 476-3437. Bimonthly Journal of Health Education is published along with the quarterly newsletter, HE-Xtra.

American College Health Association (ACHA) [1]

The American College Health Association is made up of individuals and institutions of higher education dealing with health problems and issues in academic communities. It promotes continuing education, research, and program development related to educational institutions. With the increased amount of health education programming in college and university health services, ACHA has become an important forum for health education functioning in those settings. For additional information, contact ACHA, 780 Elkridge Landing Rd., Linthicum, MD 21090, (410) 859-1500. Bimonthly journal, Journal of the American College Health Association.

American Public Health Association (APHA) [1]

The American Public Health Association is the largest and oldest membership public health organization in the United States with over 30,000 members. It represents the major disciplines and specialists related to public health from community health planning and dental health to statistics and veterinary public health. APHA has two sections of primary interest to health educators: The Public Health Education and Health Promotion Section and the School Health Education and Services Section.

The Public Health Education and Health Promotion Section is one of the larger sections of APHA. It is concerned with articulating health education roles and advocating for health education concerns throughout the overall APHA organization and its various sections and state affiliates. It is a major sponsor of scientific papers related to health education during the APHA annual meetings.

The School Health Education and Services Section advocates within the APHA structure for comprehensive school health. Such input includes the traditional areas of health instruction in schools, school health services, and healthful school environment. This section sponsors major scientific papers on school health during annual meetings of APHA.

For further information contact APHA, 1015 15th Street, NW, Suite 300, Washington, D.C. 20005, (202) 789-5600. Monthly journal, American Journal of Public Health. The monthly newsletter is Nation's Health. Both sections send out newsletters.

American School Health Association (ASHA)[1]

The American School Health Association is the primary professional organization concerned with issues related to school-age children. There are currently close to 3,000 members in the organization. School health services, healthful school environment, and comprehensive school health education are key areas of concern. ASHA provides the major forum for discussion of school health issues through annual, regional, and local affiliate meetings as well as through publications and journals. ASHA provides leadership in professional preparation and practice standards for school health educators, school nurses, physicians, and dental personnel. For further information, contact ASHA, P.O. Box 708, Kent, OH 44240, (330) 678-1601. Journal name: Journal of School Health.

American Society for Healthcare Education and Training (ASHET)

The American Society for Healthcare Education and Training is a membership organization representing a diversity of healthcare and educational organizations for the purpose of promoting awareness of the educational needs common to all healthcare personnel, continuation of professional development in management, and participation in national health issues. Health educators in medical-care settings find this organization particularly helpful. It has local chapters in large cities that present programs for professional development. The organization is linked to the American Hospital Association and can be reached at ASHET, 1 North Franklin, Chicago, IL 60606, (312) 280-6113. The journal: Journal of Healthcare Education and Training. The newsletter is now called Focal Point.

Association of State and Territorial Directors of Health Promotion and Public Health Education (ASTDHPPHE)

The Association of State and Territorial Directors of Public Health Education membership is made up of 65 directors of health education for each state and/or territory and the Indian Health Service of the U.S. The association is primarily concerned with developing standards of health education programming at the state level. It has been active recently in developing communication mechanisms on health education between state health departments and the federal government in matters related to health education. The association is an affiliate of the Association of State and Territorial Health Officials. For further information on ASTDHPPHE, contact any state department of public health or, 1015 15th Street, NW, Suite 410, Washington, D.C. 20005, (202) 289-6639. The name of their newsletter is ASTDHPPHE News.

International Union for Health Promotion Education (IUHPE)

The International Union for Health Promotion Education is an international professional organization committed to the development of health education around the world and has constituent, institutional, and individual memberships. The union cooperates closely with the World Health Organization and the United Nations Educational, Scientific, and Cultural Organization (UNESCO) in a variety of international forums. IUHPE has four major objectives aimed at improving health through education, including establishing links between organizations and people working in health education in various countries of the world, facilitating worldwide exchanges of information, promoting scientific research and improving professional preparation in health education, and promoting the development of informed public opinion. The union meets every three years for an international conference.

For more information on the Union contact the North American Regional Office/IUHPE, 1015 15th Sreet, NW, Suite 410, Washington, D.C. 20005. The quarterly journal is called <u>Health Promotion.</u>

Society for Public Health Education (SOPHE)[1]

Founded in 1950, the Society for Public Health Education has provided a major leadership role in public health education, both nationally and internationally. The society was formed to promote, encourage, and contribute to the advancement of health for all people by encouraging research, standards of professional preparation and practice, and continuing education for community and public health education. Currently there are 2,200 members. SOPHE has local chapters throughout the United States that provide continuing education and job referrals. It has articulated standards for master's-level public health educators, an approval process for baccalaureate-level academic programs in community health education, and a code of ethics that is widely cited in health literature. For further information, contact SOPHE, 1015 15th Street, NW, Suite 410, Washington, D.C. 20005, (202) 408-9804. The journal is called <u>Health Education and Behavior.</u> The quarterly newsletter is <u>SOPHE News and Views.</u>

Society of State Directors of Health, Physical Education, and Recreation (SSDHPER)[1]

The Society of State Directors of Health, Physical Education, and Recreation membership comprises directors of school health, physical education, and recreation in state agencies. Its goal is to promote comprehensive statewide programs of school health, physical education, recreation, and safety. The society works closely with the American Alliance for Health, Physical Education, Recreation, and Dance and the other members of the Coalition of National Health Education Organizations. For further information, contact any state department of education.

The Coalition of National Health Education Organizations

The coalition includes representatives from the American College Health Association (Health Education Section), APHA (Public Health Education and Health Promotion section and the School Health Education and Services section), American School Health Association, SOPHE, AAHE, ASTDHPPHE, and SSDHPER. The coalition attempts to unify the vision, standards, and objectives for the profession and ensures that health education is appropriately represented in national discussion, decisions, and policy development. The address and telephone number are in association with the current chair.

Association for Worksite Health Promotion (AWHP)

The Association for Worksite Health Promotion is a not-for-profit network of worksite health promotion professionals dedicated to sharing the best-of-practice methods, processes and technologies. Since 1974, AWHP members have been advancing their own careers through the many educational resource and recreational opportunities offered by AWHP. (*AWHP Website, 1997*) For further information, contact 60 Revere Drive, Suite 500, Northbrook, IL 60062, (847) 480-9574.

---

[1] *These organizations are represented on the National Commission for Health Education Credentialing.*

The Certified Health Education Specialist

A. SELECT COMMUNICATIONS METHODS AND TECHNIQUES

Health communications programs can increase awareness of a health issue, problem or solution, affect attitudes to create support for individual or collective action, demonstrate or illustrate skills, increase demand for health services, and remind about or reinforce knowledge, attitudes, or behavior.

Health communications programs cannot compensate for a lack of health care services, produce behavior change without supportive program components, or be equally effective in addressing all issues or relaying all messages.

Theories and models used in planning health communications programs come from social marketing, health education, and mass media. Social marketing is defined as the principles and techniques of marketing to increase effectiveness of programs aimed at producing social change. The four Ps of marketing are product, promotion, place, and price. *(Kotler, 1987)* Dever points up the relationship of epidemiology and social marketing, saying that both aim to strengthen the fit between the health services offered and the needs of the populations: "Marketing theory is based on a systemic view of organizations in which their functioning is viewed in terms of exchange." *(Dever, 1991)*

> *See page 70 for communications persuasion model.*

> *See Flora, 1989 for four major uses for mass media in health promotion: educator, promoter, supporter, supplementer.*

> *See Green, 1984 "A Macro Intervention to Support Health Behavior" for synthesis of communication models.*

Concepts

Gatekeepers or Opinion Leaders—Research on the process of personal influence suggests a movement of information through two basic stages:
First, from media to relatively well-informed individuals who frequently attend to mass communications; second, from those persons through interpersonal channels to individuals who had less direct exposure to media and who depend upon others for their information. **This is called the two-step flow of communication** and is related to the adoption of innovation concept. *(See page 89.)*

Communications models—Four roles for mass media messages in health interventions have been identified: primary change agent, complement to other interventions, means of recruitment and promotion of services and programs, and provider of support for lifestyle-health changes. *(Flora, 1989)* In large-scale information campaigns, the role of the primary change agent is paramount, particularly in geographically dispersed efforts. Media campaigns can reach large audiences quickly and efficiently and are thought to be an excellent first step in raising awareness about an issue or mobilizing a community. The other roles for media may be carried out locally in complementary tactics with minor media such as church and club newsletters, cable, or supermarket and workplace displays.

```
┌─────────────────────────────────────────────────────────────────────┐
│                 C O M M U N I C A T I O N S   S K I L L S             │
│                                                                       │
│  1. ORAL INFORMAL SKILLS... Establish rapport, listening skills —     │
│     read body language, paraphrase, give and get feedback.            │
│                                                                       │
│  2. ORAL FORMAL SKILLS... Public speaking — organization, delivery,   │
│     use of audio-visuals.                                             │
│                                                                       │
│  3. WRITTEN SKILLS... Adequate preparation, audience analysis, tone,  │
│     composition — clarity, coherence, conciseness, correctness.       │
│                                                                       │
│  4. PUBLIC RELATIONS AND MARKETING... PR concerned about images and   │
│     is a management tool. Marketing is concerned about programs and   │
│     products and works to determine what people want or need and      │
│     requires consumer rather than provider orientation. Both require  │
│     plans and knowledge of media markets, surveying, focus group      │
│     testing, publicity, and design.                                   │
│     Criterion: Health educators should maintain liaison with media    │
│     representatives to coordinate and ensure accurate and timely      │
│     distribution of information via newspapers, TV, radio, and other  │
│     media sources. (Standards of Practice, 1991)                      │
│                                                                       │
│  5. MASS MEDIA... Know uses, limitations, timing, and scope.          │
└─────────────────────────────────────────────────────────────────────┘
```

Health media efforts are becoming more sophisticated and have moved from public service to paid accounts and to advocacy and enter-education.

Media advocacy is the strategic use of mass media as a resource for advancing social or public policy initiative. Positive issue advocacy and negation of the disinformation activities of adversaries occur when the media becomes the arena for contesting public policies. There is a role for paid media (advertising) in media advocacy. Limitations of funding and the pervasiveness of unpaid media (news) in the shaping of public perception of issues make the news media the primary arena for media advocacy. (NCI, 1988)

"Enter-education" or "edutainment" combines entertainment and education to bring about positive changes in attitudes and behavior. Enter-education influences social norms and fits with media's powerful effect in transmission of culture. Examples are discussing condom use, refusing a cigarette, or designating a driver for a party as embedded in TV sitcoms, soap operas, or MTV. (Steckler, 1995)

GLOSSARY OF
COMMUNICATION
TERMS
from "Making Health
Communication
Programs Work"

Attention. A pretesting measure to describe a message's ability to attract listener or viewer attention; this is often called "recall."

Attitudes. An individual's predispositions toward an object, person, or group, that influence his or her response to be either positive or negative, favorable or unfavorable, etc.

Baseline study. The collection and analysis of data regarding a target audience or situation prior to intervention.

Central location intercept interviews. Interviews conducted with respondents who are stopped at a highly trafficked location that is frequented by individuals typical of the desired target audience.

Channel. The route of message delivery (e.g., mass media, community, interpersonal).

Closed-ended questions. Questions that provide respondents with a list of possible answers from which to choose; also called multiple choice questions.

Communication concepts. Rough art work and statements that convey the idea for a full message.

Communication strategy statement. A written statement that includes program objectives, target audiences, an understanding of the information needs and perceptions of each target audience, what actions they should take, the reasons why they should act, and the benefits to be gained. This document provides the direction and consistency for all program messages and materials.

Comparison group. A control group randomly selected and matched to the target population according to characteristics identified in the study to permit a comparison of changes between those who receive the intervention and those who do not.

Comprehension. A pretesting measure to determine whether messages are clearly understood.

Convenience samples. Samples that consist of respondents who are typical of the target audience and who are easily accessible; not statistically projectable to the entire population being studied.

Diagnostic information. Results from pretesting research that indicate the strengths and weaknesses in messages and materials.

Focus group interviews. A type of qualitative research in which an experienced moderator leads about 8 or 10 respondents through a discussion of a selected topic, allowing them to talk freely and spontaneously.

Formative evaluation. Evaluative research conducted during program development. May include state-of-the-art reviews, pretesting messages and materials, and pilot testing a program on a small scale before full implementation.

Frequency. In advertising, is used to describe the average number of times an audience is exposed to a specific media message.

Gatekeeper. Someone you must work with before you can reach a target audience (e.g., a schoolteacher) or accomplish a task (e.g., a television public service director).

Goal. The overall improvement the program will strive to create.

Impact evaluation. Research designed to identify whether and to what extent a program contributed to accomplishing its stated goals (here, more global than outcome evaluation).

In-depth interviews. A form of qualitative research consisting of intensive interviews to find out how people think and what they feel about a given topic.

Intermediaries. Organizations, such as professional, industrial, civic, social or fraternal groups, that act as channels for distributing program messages and materials to members of the desired target audience.

Objective. A quantifiable statement of a desired program achievement necessary to reach a program goal.

Open-ended questions. Questions that allow an individual to respond freely in his or her own words.

Outcome evaluation. Research designed to account for a program's accomplishments and effectiveness; also called "impact" evaluation.

Over-recruiting. Recruiting more respondents than required to compensate for expected "no-shows."

Polysyllabic words. Words that contain three or more syllables.

Pretesting. A type of formative research that involves systematically gathering target audience reactions to messages and materials before they are produced in final form.

Probe. Interviewer techniques used to solicit additional information about a question or issue. Probe should be neutral (e.g., "What else can you tell me about _____?"), not directive ("Do you think the pamphlet was suggesting that you take a particular step, such as changing your diet?").

Process evaluation. Evaluation to study the components of program implementation; includes assessments of whether materials are being distributed to the right people and in what quantities, whether and to what extent program activities are occurring, and other measures of how and how well the program is working.

PSA. Public service announcement, used without charge by the media.

HEALTH EDUCATION IN SCHOOL SETTINGS

1. Which of the following is the most important factor in an individual's use of self-control techniques for maintaining a behavioral change?
    a) Independence from formal intervention
    b) Ability to measure the behavioral change
    c) Follow-up at regular intervals
    d) Intrinsic motivation and self-reliance

2. Which group is most influential in planning school health education content?
    a) Teachers
    b) Parents
    c) State legislators
    d) School nurses

3. The best approach to fostering an individual's responsibility for a positive lifestyle change is to:
    a) Schedule annual medical examinations
    b) Provide brochures about health topics
    c) Develop a personal behavioral contract
    d) View videos on health-related conditions

4. The theoretical base or model offering a wide range of interventions for planning behavior changes is:
    a) Health belief
    b) Social learning
    c) Diffusion of innovations
    d) Stages of change

5. The best role models for behavior and attitude change regarding teen pregnancy prevention are:
    a) School nurses
    b) Teachers
    c) Peer counselors
    d) Community volunteers

6. Which one of the following is not one of the three major components of the comprehensive school health model?
    a) Healthful environment
    b) Health administration
    c) Health education
    d) Health services

DEFINITIONS
Joint Committee on Terminology 1990

Comprehensive School Health Program — An organized set of policies, procedures, and activities designed to protect and promote the health and well-being of students and staff that has traditionally included health services, healthful school environment, and health education. It should also include, but not be limited to, guidance and counseling, physical education, food service, social work, psychological services, and employee health promotion.

School Health Education — One component of the comprehensive school health program that includes the development, delivery, and evaluation of a planned instructional program and other activities for students preschool through grade 12, for parents, and for school staff and is designed to influence positively the health knowledge, attitudes, and skills of individuals.

Comprehensive School Health Instruction — The development, delivery, and evaluation of a planned curriculum, preschool through 12, with goals, objectives, content sequence, and specific classroom lessons that includes, but is not limited to, the following major content areas: community health, consumer health, environmental health, family life, mental and emotional health, injury prevention and safety, nutrition, personal health, prevention and control of disease, and substance use and abuse.

Postsecondary Health Education Program — A planned set of health education policies, procedures, activities, and services that are directed to students, faculty, and/or staff of colleges, universities, and other higher education institutions. This includes, but is not limited to general health courses for students, employee and student health promotion activities, health services, professional preparation of health educators and other professionals, self-help groups, and student life.

PURPOSE — Protect, maintain, and promote the health of the children and adults who live and work together every day of the school year. Schools must maintain the health of students to ensure continued fitness to learn, maintain an environment that contributes to health, do their best to ensure optimum health through appropriate health services, and educate children to make sound decisions on health-related matters. Wellness-oriented, comprehensive, sequentially organized health instruction makes a strong, effective program. *(Kane, 1993)*

The Certified Health Education Specialist

PROCESSES — The goal is comprehensive school programs integrating health instruction, services, and environment. Health teaching must be integrated into all appropriate areas of curriculum. Work with families. Adults in schools provide models for behaviors. Some schools are beginning to provide health promotion programs for staff and teachers. Community practices interact and overlap with schools. The focus is on curriculum development and teaching skills, along with health content.

ASSESSMENT — The target group for school health is kids, a captive audience. They are mostly healthy, which makes for a positive approach as opposed to a disease or problem focus. The school administrators are the decision makers for school health programs. Federal, state, and local policies and resources influence the status as do community needs and pressures. Interview administrators, parents, students, and teachers when determining curriculum. Needs assessment determines the scope and sequence of the curriculum. Link health-related behavioral problems and solutions to age groups and to cultural groups. Analyze students' health beliefs based on Health Belief Model, Piaget's Cognitive Development Theory. The elementary teacher is the critical provider for health instruction. Tools used: records including student files, cumulative records; interviews with parents, administrators, teachers, school nurse; surveys, community data.

PLAN — Equip children with fundamental health concepts and problem-solving skills that will lead to sound decision making in the future. State and local health and safety codes must be considered. School policies impact health instruction. The sources of school health education curriculum are based on answers to basic questions about goals, changes, and methods.

IMPLEMENT — Classroom teachers deliver the health education in elementary schools. Some health-trained teachers are found in junior and senior high schools. School nurses are critical. Curriculum development, instructional skills, and small group discussion skills are major needs in classrooms.

EVALUATE — Assess needs that help determine the scope and emphasis of health instruction, assess strengths and weaknesses of the program (process), and assess the extent to which desired outcomes are attained (impact). Emphasize pre/post-tests. Use evaluation data formatively as a basis for revisions in course methodology. Few school programs are able to follow up and assess long-range outcomes, except for specially funded programs. Many in school health believe that teachers and schools can be held accountable only for students' health knowledge and skills.

COORDINATE — Identify, organize and coordinate school and community resources used in health instruction programs. Synchronize with voluntary agencies and community health campaigns to multiply effect.

RESOURCES — Select community resources not in conflict with school point of view. Select resources suitable to the maturity level of the learner. Choose materials that contain valid health content and concepts. Identify school and community resources that can enrich health instruction. Accumulate and organize health materials, contacts, and sources.

COMMUNICATE — Models appreciation of health values and zest for living. Sensitive to needs of learners and health levels of students. Delivers messages that are not too sophisticated or too mundane.

ISSUES — Local control over organized curricula; states prescribe subjects at what grade level but not always for health education. Community control and concern over content. Teaching values and morals is most controversial, particularly related to sexuality education. Finding funding for faculty positions in health education, finding time for health instruction, and finding teaching staff that are health specialists are problems for administrators seeking to implement comprehensive school health education programs.

ROLES — Develop and evaluate curricula for health; classroom teacher implements health curriculum developed by others; health educator content specialist and trainer; community health educators serve as subject matter experts, curriculum consultants, resource brokers, coordinators, and role models.

For universities and colleges, and professional organizations, roles are instructor, consultant, evaluator, student health organizer, coordinator, and disseminator of information.

HEALTH EDUCATION IN COMMUNITY SETTINGS

1. You are a consultant in a voluntary organization and see some unethical behavior among employees. Whom do you notify?
   a) The executive director
   b) The consultee
   c) The board of directors
   d) The direct supervisor of the employee

2. Most health-related voluntary agencies are established and based on:
   a) A single major health problem or a body organ
   b) A priority stated in **Healthy People 2000**
   c) A state law or mandate
   d) A service delivery concern

3. Program planning for a community health department begins with an assessment of existing:
   a) Health personnel resources
   b) Community health agencies
   c) Local health department resources
   d) Health needs, concerns, and assets

4. You are the health educator for the American Dental Association. Your program includes the following objectives: the participants will adopt positive attitudes toward tooth brushing; the participants will rate daily brushing as a highly important activity; the participants will demonstrate correct use of a toothbrush. These are:
   a) Behavioral objectives
   b) Process objectives
   c) Outcome objectives
   d) Impact objectives

5. The adoption curve illustrates:
   a) A prediction of the amount of time it takes to integrate a new idea within an ethnic group
   b) The early adopters are healthier and smarter than late adopters
   c) The effectiveness of mass media on multiple populations
   d) The successive waves of use by groups with identifiable characteristics

6. The perception of the constituency group in the Social Action Model of community organization is that they are:
   a) Citizens who can use self-help methods
   b) Consumers who need facts
   c) Residents who are victims of the system
   d) Early adopters of innovative strategies

PURPOSE — Reduce the incidence of health problems or improve the health status of the community including improving access, changing policies and legislation, shifting community norms, and affecting specific behaviors.

Encouraging public participation is more than requesting input; it allows public access to the decision-making process, seeks community solutions for institutionalized change, and achieves partnerships by sharing resources and decision-making power. *(Standards of Practice, 1991)*

DEFINITION — *(Joint Committee on Terminology, 1990)*

Community health education is the application of a variety of methods that result in the education and mobilization of community members in actions for resolving health issues and problems that affect the community. These methods include, but are not limited to, group process, mass media, communication, community organization, organization development, strategic planning, skills training, legislation, policy making, and advocacy.

Bracht identifies themes about the process of community-based social and behavioral change. (1) Powerful social forces influence individual behavior; behavior formed and influenced by the dominant culture shapes individual behavior symbolically and tangibly and transmits values and norms. (2) Communities can be mobilized as a change agent to achieve social and behavioral change. Each community is unique but processes to be followed in analysis, design, organization, implementation, and diffusion of programs are similar. (3) Early and sustained participation by community members and leaders is necessary for realization of community ownership and program maintenance. *(Bracht, 1990)*

Green distinguishes between community interventions that seek small but pervasive changes which apply to the majority of the population on a community-wide approach and interventions in a community that seek more intensive or profound change in a subpopulation, such as a school or workplace. The differences are the comparative magnitude of the task and the number of organizations and levels of organization involved. *(Green, 1991)*

Community organization outcomes are independent entities working for a mutual goal; promotion of cooperation rather than competition among groups; coordination of existing resources; shared leadership, talent, and responsibilities; collaboration and negotiation; and community input into decision making. *(Standards of Practice, 1991)*

THREE MODELS OF COMMUNITY PRACTICE *(Ross, 1974)*

Community Development — Change through broad community participation and consensus to develop community capacity, integration, and self-help for economic and social progress. The clients or targets are the citizens and the power structure are collaborators. The health educator role is catalyst/coordinator.

Social Planning — Change through technical process of problem solving (use consensus or conflict). Rational, controlled change is central. Use experts and data, clients are seen as consumers, power structure are employers and sponsors. The health educator acts as fact gatherer, analyst, and facilitator.

Social Action — Organization of disadvantaged segment, perhaps with alliances to make demands on larger community for resources or justice (conflict model). Aims to redistribute

The Certified Health Education Specialist

power, resources, basic policies of formal organizations. Clients perceived as victims. Health educator role is partisan activist, agitator, negotiator.

PROCESSES — Increased community competence or problem-solving ability is a defining characteristic of a community organization process. *(Ross, 1974)* Principle of participation critical in assessment and planning, not just in implementation of programs at this level. The relevant principle is "starting where people are." Processes of collaboration (when one or more organizations perceive that their own goals can be achieved most effectively and efficiently with the assistance and the resources of others) and negotiation (organization holds discussions with those who evidence varying degrees of resistance to the redistribution of power or resources in the hope of ultimately arriving at an agreement).

ASSESSMENT — Coalition building essential; multilayer assessments, epidemiological, political, economic, sociological, and behavioral; use data sources (see Assessment Section) and interpersonal processes.

Tools: influentials and informants (interview key people), surveys, focus groups, records, census, and epidemiological data analysis.

PLAN — Sequencing of activities critical, use of multiple intervention strategies both environmental forces and behavioral patterns, mass media, coalition building, training, skill building, use of existing organizations and resources. Anticipate resistance to change.

IMPLEMENT — Partnerships, participation, coalitions, training, technical assistance, small group dynamics. Development of task forces; development of social system support; organizational commitment to an improved social environment. Track and monitor activity development.

EVALUATE — Plan for evaluation at initial planning stage. Evidence that participation goals are being met, that behavior change strategies are working, and that efforts are paying off. Short-term results, changes in policies, allocations, community norms documented and communicated. Long-term effects require access to epidemiological and community records for comparison and/or baseline data. Plan progress reports, disseminate results to those feeling ownership, interest, or who are affected by the problem.

COORDINATE — Coordinate with community agencies if resources are included in plan or with other health campaigns for synergism; major nonhealth attention-getters in community — holidays, drives, campaigns, etc.

RESOURCES — See Processes above on negotiation and collaboration.

COMMUNICATE — Plan for dissemination of information, creation of climate, and adoption of innovation through mass media, minor media, small groups, and organizations.

ISSUES —Size of program, politics, power, and collaboration.

The theory of adoption of innovation and diffusion through a population summarizes what is known about how changes progress through a community. It provides a framework for orchestrating (segmenting, sequencing, and timing) methods to maximize the spread of the adoption of the change throughout the community.

An innovation is an idea or practice that is perceived as new by an individual or group. The idea is not necessarily new but perceived as new by the unit of adoption. This definition also includes programs. *(Rogers, 1983)* Usually adoption of programs involves organizational change, which increases the opportunity for a greater number of individuals to be exposed to the health program. *(Parcel, 1990)* Models of organizational diffusion have been proposed but are not yet applied in general practice.

Adoption of a new idea moves through groups. Early groups of adopters are different from later groups and their economic and attitudinal characteristics can be categorized with different interventions indicated for different groups. Groups in higher socially stratified levels are usually early adopters.

The rates of change vary at different stages and are predictable. Relative rates of change early in the introduction of a new program will be slow, but as the program progresses the rate of change in the population will speed up until it has included the majority of potential consumers. Then the rate of change will become slower as the program attempts to reach the more socially isolated and more resistant subgroups. *(Green, 1978)*

Initiation of diffusion may be centralized in one agency and move outward and down, or it may originate with a network or local organization and move upward and outward. When information is intended for an entire community, both types of systems should be activated because they serve complementary functions.

Given the concern for adoption, implementation, and long-term viability (institutionalization) to maintain changes that have been achieved, diffusion is a critical issue. For the spread to take hold, programs must have sufficient impact and be allowed sufficient time to make a difference.

Stages of Change

New behavior does not emerge at once but from a continuous series of steps. Individual stages proposed in the Transtheoretical Model *(Prochaska, 1986)* include: precontemplation — no interest, not considering change; contemplation — serious thought given to change; preparation — getting ready with skills and emotional attitudes; action — overt action tried and evaluated; maintenance — period when behavior is continued and becomes habit, or when relapse occurs and the process is recycled.

DEFINITIONS — Participation/involvement: A process in which individuals or communities identify with a movement and take responsibility jointly with health professionals and others concerned for making decisions and planning and carrying out activities. Community organization is "a health education process or method in which the combined efforts of individuals, groups, and organizations are designed to generate, mobilize, coordinate, utilize, and/or redistribute resources to meet unsolved or emergent health needs or problems." *(Ross, 1967)*

ROLES —

Health departments: Enforcement and education components as communications specialists — planning interventions that combine community organization, organizational development, group process, communication; advocacy for policies and legislation, work with a variety of departments and specialties such as nurses or environmentalists.

State and federal: Work with other agencies as constituents, grant writing and monitoring communications. Resource development and training.

Voluntary agencies: Professional education, public education, supervision and training of volunteers, resource development, and materials development.

**Figure 14
THE
CUMULATIVE
ADOPTION CURVE**
(Rogers, 1983)

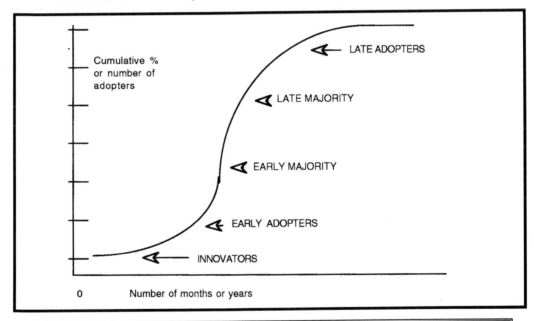

DESCRIPTION OF ADOPTERS

INNOVATORS   VENTURESOME
EARLY ADOPTERS   RESPECTABLE
EARLY MAJORITY   DELIBERATE
LATE MAJORITY   SKEPTICAL
LAGGARDS   TRADITIONAL

HEALTH EDUCATION IN WORKSITE/OCCUPATIONAL SETTINGS

1. Aggregate Health Risk Assessment (HRA) data are used to:
   a) Set health insurance rates
   b) Evaluate effectiveness of health promotion programs
   c) Determine health promotion cost-effectiveness
   d) Plan programs specific to a workplace

2. Individual HRA data summaries can be used to:
   a) Determine health promotion cost-effectiveness
   b) Counsel employees on lifestyle change
   c) Set health insurance rates
   d) Evaluate effectiveness of health promotion programs

3. How can you tell that employees are interested in a voluntary smoking cessation program?
   a) The number of employees who smoke according to a self-report survey
   b) The attendance at an orientation meeting for stop-smoking classes
   c) Response to an employer's interview
   d) The vote of the health promotion planning committee

4. You are responsible for determining an intervention to deal with the absenteeism and alcoholism problems identified by a health risk assessment in a corporation. Which one of the following is the most appropriate program to address these problems?
   a) A crisis intervention program
   b) An Alcoholics Anonymous program
   c) A stress management program
   d) An employee assistance program

5. A worksite health promotion planning committee will be most effective if it:
   a) Has financial support from management
   b) Is allowed to meet on company time
   c) Has limited responsibilities
   d) Reflects the diversity of employment in the company

PURPOSE — Specifically, raise morale, reduce absenteeism, and reduce unintentional injury or utilization of health care. Also, enhance productivity of workers, reduce employer medical costs, bottom line enhance profitability. (Business is a major purchaser of health care through worker/retiree health insurance.)

PROCESSES — Relevance, quality, accessibility, and affordability are key concerns; participation of workers and union with management critical in planning and implementing. Organizational assessment of corporate culture important. Internal marketing critical. Must enlist support of upper management.

ASSESSMENT — Health Risk Assessment/Appraisal useful. *(See page 22)*
Also assess policies, structures, and type of industry that create constraints. Medical professionals maintain records that can be used to identify health needs of workers. Employers and unions are important to include. Health promotion priorities generally are reduce smoking, reduce alcohol and drug misuse, improve diet and nutrition, increase physical fitness and exercise, and manage stress and violence, in that order. Occupational safety issues are generally not perceived as health education turf.

PLAN — Fit into existing company structure. Targets vary— workers, dependents, retirees. Comprehensiveness is variable. Time allotted— clock time or worker time. Facilities vary. In-house or community resource use. Consider incentives, competitions, or rewards.

IMPLEMENT — Need advisory groups for feedback and adaptation. Continuous communication of results to participants and management. Ways to ration scarce resources: wait list or screen participants, self-help referral to community resources, and stepped-up programs of intervention.

EVALUATE — Plan for evaluation at planning stage. Evidence that participation goals are being met, that behavior change strategies are working, and that investments are paying off. Short-term results quantified and communicated. Long-term effects require access to personnel, medical, or insurance records for comparison. Plan progress reports; disseminate results.

COORDINATE — Internal departmental coordination needed. Yearly company calendar must coordinate with activities. Coordinate with community agencies if resources are included in plan.

RESOURCES — Total company support to worker-supported activities.

COMMUNICATE — Critical to have marketing plan at initiation, continuous monitoring and reporting to management and to workers, plus motivational materials.

ETHICAL ISSUES — Confidentiality of records, conflicting loyalties, behavior change vs. environmental/hazard change; labeling and coercion of individuals, "victim blaming"; overly optimistic, misrepresentation of benefits to be derived; unintentional consequences such as discrimination in hiring or compromising medical care benefits. Discrimination against older workers because they use more health care.

ISSUES — Cost benefit data are critical. Starting with pilot program to demonstrate effectiveness good tactic. Participation of workers a major problem. Focus on worker behavior rather than environmental stresses and hazards problematic. Should focus on both for best program.

ROLES — Plan, implement, evaluate programs; disseminate materials, market to generate management and participant support; facilitate group process and educational assessment skills; budget, evaluation, quality assurance.
   Implementor of specific components: adult education skills, motivational skills, materials development, reporting and recording, and content specialty.

HEALTH EDUCATION IN HEALTH-CARE SETTINGS

1. The concept that individuals are likely to engage in health-promoting actions when they perceive their identified risk as serious and that they are personally susceptible, is a basic assumption of the:
   a) Health Belief Model
   b) PRECEDE/PROCEED Model
   c) Self-Help Model
   d) Cognitive Action Model

2. You are the health educator for the clinic that generated the data shown on the clinical cases graph below, representing 113 women. How would you respond to the immediate demand for an educational program by the head of the clinic?
   a) Assure him/her that you will put it in the budget request for next year
   b) Gather data to identify the existence of a behavioral component in the problem
   c) Secure epidemiological and target group data to find out whether this is an episodic chance occurrence or a new trend
   d) Request assistance from the health department epidemiologist

3. The same graph also indicates infections among a cohort of women and shows the monthly number of new cases of a diagnosed asymptomatic infection and the cumulative number of cases at the end of 6 months. Pick the correct statement from the following:
   a) The incidence is higher every month
   b) The prevalence is variable every month
   c) The prevalence has risen steadily each month
   d) The infectious cases identified show that they have been cured within ten days of diagnosis

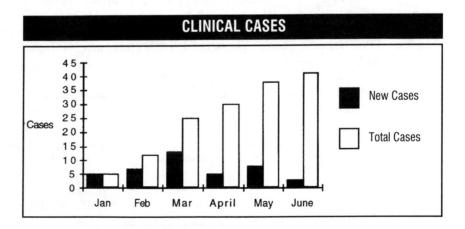

4. *Your hospital has contracted with the state health department to provide health services to a rural community. A group of new immigrants in the community have an outbreak of measles among their children. They resist immunization. Your job is to develop an education and recruitment campaign quickly to forestall a serious epidemic. You have been unable to develop relationships with this target group beyond minimal contacts and do not have the time to build trust by systematic increments. From the following, select the best alternative step for needs assessment:*
   a) Develop a database of epidemiologic and other records
   b) Relate to and enlist groups that work with the target group
   c) Define the problem, identify an action, and enlist a spokesperson within the target group to relate to the group
   d) Call the state health department for advice

PURPOSE — Health care systems are concerned with keeping their consumers/enrollees well (primary prevention), identifying problems early through detection, diagnosis, and treatment, (secondary prevention) and slowing the progress of illness, avoiding complications and enhancing the quality of life. When purchasers of care (mainly insurance companies, governments, and employers) provide a fixed sum per capita to provide health care for an identified population, it is now called Managed Care. The major concerns of the health care system providers are quality of care and consumer satisfaction. In many organizations emphasis is also on reducing utilization of services and building self-reliance through self-help, since the organization will lose money if patients use too many services. The term for this focus is "demand management."

Health promotion/health education focuses on access and utilization of services, referral to community resources and building partnerships with community education resources, developing appropriate methods and materials, training providers and staff who are in contact with the patients, and, in some cases, teaching classes.

PROCESSES — The focus is on the specific population, geographical, economic bracket, an industry such as teachers, or age groups such as seniors or young mothers with children. It can be potential consumers who are marketing targets, who have already enrolled in a group, or who use the hospital or ER. The health educator identifies the barriers that hinder or the facilitators that assist in reaching the goals of the agency.

ASSESSMENT — Hospital and clinic records (utilization, discharge data, readmissions), patient and provider surveys, community surveys, and marketing surveys are data sources. Concerns of medical personnel are important.

Tools: interested party analysis (interview key people), questionnaire checklist, focus groups, structured interviews, community data, tracking patient through system, or conducting systems analysis.

PLAN — List all behaviors affecting the particular solution and determine whether policy, structure, organizational constraints, or specific programmatic approaches will influence provider or patient behavior. Determine which behaviors are most important in affecting health status; determine which behaviors are the easiest to change, given a limited amount of educational time. Focus on skill development, not just on knowledge of disease, at patient level. Family and peer support is important for new patient behaviors.

METHODS — Use national media and local media to develop climate for change if programs are available, computer-based education for specific health problems, films/videotapes, brainstorming, role playing, rehearsal, questioning, self monitoring, contracting. One-to-one education, which is the most common type, has four major considerations: time available, knowing what to teach, knowing how to teach, and documenting what has been taught. Redmon identifies major differences between learning models used in schools vs. patient education; the goals of cognitive skill and discipline-orientation in school are replaced in patient education by teaching independent problem solving in an irregular time frame. *(Redmon, 1981)* No single channel of education is inherently superior to another, and the effectiveness of specific interventions depends on their appropriate selection and application. *(Mullen, 1990)*

IMPLEMENT — Documentation, tracking and monitoring, legal requirements for accreditation. Alternative to patient record is patient check-off list. Training for providers continuous.

EVALUATE — Effectiveness measures depend on level of planning; range from morbidity and mortality at institution level to improved utilization, compliance, health status at program level to specific skills, attitudes, and behaviors at patient level.

COORDINATE — Must coordinate delivery of programs with inflexible demands and time tables of medical institutions.

RESOURCES — Community, voluntary agency, and commercial resources can be found for educational materials and services. Be sure to pretest materials and check on most current information.

COMMUNICATE — Patient recruitment depends on marketing to the health professionals and encouraging referrals. Marketing to public depends on making program attractive, affordable, right time, and accessible.

ETHICS — Atmosphere of medical institution intimidating and coercive to patients; difficult to encourage self-management and self-determination.

ISSUES — Adherence or compliance to prescribed regimen, drug interactions, physician-patient interactions. Three strategies to increase adherence to regimen: Correct patients' misconceptions about the regimen, adjust the intervention to patients' lifestyles, and enhance support from family members. The role of the health education specialist vs. provider of service is based on role identification and role responsibilities – health education overall planning, implementation and evaluation of education programs, provider usually one-to-one counseling.

ROLES — Development of community awareness, patient support networks, professional education initiatives. As directors, managers, coordinators of programs, focus is often administrative and supportive rather than educational. As education specialists, curriculum developer, plan, implement, and evaluate programs, select methods and materials, and be a staff trainer. As program manager, coordinate teaching assignments and materials, carry out needs assessments and program evaluations, budget, report, and plan staff development, employee wellness, and worksite health promotion.

The National Commission for Health Education Credentialing, Inc.

For information about certification, eligibility requirements, or examination fees, locations, and scheduling, write to the commission at the following address: NCHEC, Inc., 944 Marcon Blvd., Suite 310, Allentown, PA 18103.

A Brief Introduction

The National Commission for Health Education Credentialing, Inc. (NCHEC) came into being in 1988 when a previously incorporated entity, The National Task Force on the Preparation and Practice of Health Educators, Inc., changed its name. The task force had originally been formed by the representatives of eight health education organizations concerned with articulating a clear professional identity and defining a common core of professional preparation for the field of health education.

The steps from 1977 to the present by which the task force, now the commission, defined the professional field and produced a Competency-Based Curriculum Framework, CBCF are detailed elsewhere. *(Cleary, 1995) (Pollock, 1996)*

Briefly, eight health education organizations led by SOPHE formed the original Task Force; after preliminary meetings, a Workshop on Commonalities and Differences in the Preparation and Practice of Community, Patient, and School Health Educators was held in 1978 where formation of guidelines for professional preparation in all health education settings was recommended. The next step, the Role Delineation Project, specified the responsibilities and functions, skills, and knowledge of entry-level health educators. A national survey provided the basis for role verification and refinement. A meeting of representatives from institutions preparing professional health educators was called in 1981. Revisions and clarification continued and a Framework for the Development of Competency-Based Curricula for Entry-Level Health Educators was developed and disseminated through a series of 12 regional workshops. The framework is the basis for the credentialing process as indicated below in the explanation of the examination.

The NCHEC is governed by a board of commissioners elected by certified health education specialists. The executive director is William B. Cosgrove, M.S., M.P.H., CHES. The commission is divided into three division boards with the following functions:

> Division Board for the Certification of Health Education Specialists; responsible for the CHES examination
>
> Division Board for Professional Preparation; works with colleges and universities on preparation and training
>
> Division Board for Professional Development; responsible for policies and procedures related to continuing education opportunities for the Certified Health Education Specialist.

Construction Of The Health Education Specialist Certification Examination

Construction of the Health Education Specialist Certification Examination.
(adapted from E. Tyler, the Division Coordinator's CHES Bulletin article)

The goal of certification is the development of an examination that will accurately measure practice-related knowledge and skills. The first step is to formulate a "role delineation." A role delineation is a careful description of the job duties and of the knowledge and skills needed to perform these duties. That information is used in each step of the examination development process, including the development of test specifications (content outline), construction of specific items (questions) to be included in the exam, and the composition of the examination.

Item (question) development involves two processes, the construction of items and the review of content. Items are solicited from practitioners in the field or in an item-writing workshop. Item writers are volunteers who must be CHES, represent an area of practice, and be aware of geographical variations in practice. The Professional Examination Service (PES), the organization which administers and scores the test, has developed item-writing principles that must be used in item writing.

Submitted to PES, the items are reviewed by consultants who are experts in the field and reviewed by three subject matter specialists. The items that survive are placed in a computerized item bank for possible future use in an examination.

The Division Board for the Certification of Health Education Specialists and a PES psychometrician participate in the exam construction workshop where a portion of the items previously developed that most clearly represent the test specifications are selected to be included in the first draft. The draft exam is reviewed by PES psychometricians and editors. These additional reviews enhance the quality and accuracy of the items in the exam.

A statistical procedure known as equating is used to establish the pass point. By using equating methods to link pass points across different forms of the exam, it assures that the standard of performance applied to the test results will be functionally equivalent from year to year.

The development of the exam is a complex process, taking more than a year to complete and requiring the involvement and expertise of many.

The certification examination and the entire certification process is based solely upon the competencies and subcompetencies of the framework. Exam questions are developed from the framework. If they begin from any other starting point, the exam becomes unhooked from the framework and the role delineation process in its entirety is compromised.

Cleary, H.P. The Credentialing of Health Educators: An Historical Account 1970-1990. The National Commission for Health Education Credentialing, Inc., 1995.

Pollock, Marion B. and William Carlyon. "Seven Responsibilities and How They Grew: The Story of a Curriculum Framework." Journal of Health Education, 27:2 (1996).

Tyler, E. Construction of the Health Education Specialist Certification Examination. CHES Bulletin, NCHEC, Inc., Allentown, PA, Fall 1995.

NCHEC. A Competency-Based Framework for Professional Development of Certified Health Education Specialists. National Commission for Health Education Credentialing, Inc., Allentown, PA, 1996.

THE TEST SPECIFICATIONS DOCUMENT

The Test Specifications Document that follows is linked to the seven responsibilities and related competencies that are outlined in detail in <u>A Competency-Based Framework for Professional Development of Certified Health Education Specialists.</u> *(NCHEC, 1996)* Each of the seven responsibilities is categorized into three basic sections: 1) Practice Statements, which are designated by a two-digit code; 2) Task Statements, which are designated by a four-digit code; and 3) Knowledge Statements, which are designated by a six-digit code. The Knowledge Statements are the basis for the Certification Examination and will greatly assist your self-analysis, as well as serve as a detailed review document for the examination.

THE TEST SPECIFICATIONS DOCUMENT

Practice Domains of the Areas of Responsibility

Practice Statement ▸ 01 ASSESS INDIVIDUAL AND COMMUNITY NEEDS FOR HEALTH EDUCATION

Test Statement ▸ 0101   Assess environmental factors (such as social, cultural, political, economic, physical) by gathering health-related data in order to identify health needs.

Knowledge Statement ▸ 010101   Sources of social, physical, political, cultural and economic information (e.g., morbidity, vitality reports, health statistics, epidemiology, health records, census data, zoning laws, legal codes, current research publications, ERIC).

Knowledge Statement ▸ 010102   Characteristics of valid and reliable data-gathering instruments (e.g., surveys, interview protocols) and techniques (e.g., observation, discussion groups).

0102   Assess individual and group characteristics by gathering health-related data in order to identify health needs, interests, and concerns.

010201   Sources of social, physical, political, cultural, and economic information.
010202   Characteristics of valid and reliable data-gathering instruments.
010203   Health risk appraisals.
010204   Psychosocial assessment instruments (e.g., self concept scales).
010205   Physical, social, emotional, and intellectual factors influencing health behaviors.
010206   Behaviors that tend to promote or compromise health.
010207   Theories underlying change (e.g., learning theory, change theory, social learning).

0103   Assess community and/or individual resources by gathering information in order to determine the feasibility of a health education program.

010301   Sources of social, physical, political, cultural, and economic information.
010302   Characteristics of valid and reliable data-gathering instruments.
010303   Health risk appraisals.
010304   Psychosocial assessment instruments.
010307   Theories underlying change.
010308   Available health education services.

0104   Interpret assessment and summarize assessment by analyzing environmental, individual, and group resource data in order to determine priorities for program development.

010409   Gaps and overlaps in the provision of collaborative health services.
010410   Communication techniques.
010411   Methods of reporting data (e.g., graphs, charts, tables).
010437   Statistical techniques and terms.

02 PLAN EFFECTIVE HEALTH EDUCATION PROGRAMS

0201 Collaborate with community agencies and individuals by coordinating resources and services in order to develop an effective health education plan.

020110 Communication techniques.
020117 The importance of societal value systems (e.g., cultural differences) in program planning.
020112 Strategies for identifying and involving community organizations, resources, and potential participants for support and assistance in program planning.
020113 Social, cultural, and political structures.
020114 Practical modes of collaboration.
020115 Group dynamics.
020125 Methods of conflict resolution (e.g., negotiations, confrontations).
020134 Characteristics of different organizations (e.g., public, voluntary, professional).
020138 Roles of health and related professionals.

0202 Collaborate with potential participants by involving them in the planning process in order to develop a plan acceptable to the participants.

020212 Strategies for identifying and involving community organizations, resources, and participants.
020215 Group dynamics.
020213 Social, cultural, and political structures.
020216 Strategies for dealing with controversial health issues.
020217 The importance of societal value systems (e.g., cultural differences) in program planning.

0203 Develop a health education plan to meet health needs by applying theory from such fields as psychology, sociology, education, and biology and integrating the assessment data, community resources and services, and input from potential participants.

020307 Theories underlying change.
020318 The elements of a health education program (e.g., framework, scope and sequence, goals, objectives, time line, budget, evaluation, resources).
020319 Characteristics (e.g., measurability) of program objectives.
020320 Health education learning activities and their appropriateness for objectives, and alternative educational methods (e.g., lectures, small group discussion, multimedia).
020321 Educational resources (e.g., audiovisual equipment, computers, curriculum) and criteria for selection (e.g., age and culture appropriateness, readability, learning style).
020336 Code of ethics of the profession.
020337 Statistical techniques and terms.

03 IMPLEMENT HEALTH EDUCATION PROGRAMS

0301   Implement the health education plan by employing health education methods and techniques in order to achieve program objectives.

030118   The elements of a health education program.
030119   Characteristics of program objectives.
030120   Health education learning activities.
030121   Educational resources and criteria for selection.
030122   Program management techniques and principles (e.g., supervision, staying within budget).
030123   Strategies for conducting in-service training programs.
030136   Code of ethics for the profession.

04 EVALUATE EFFECTIVENESS OF HEALTH EDUCATION PROGRAMS

0401   Develop a program evaluation plan by establishing criteria of effectiveness in order to assess the achievement of program objectives.

040102   Characteristics of valid and reliable data-gathering instruments.
040103   Health risk appraisals.
040104   Psychosocial assessment instruments.
040111   Methods of reporting data.
040124   Application of evaluations (e.g., formative, process, program outcome, summative, cost effectiveness, impact, outcome).

0402   Monitor the health education program by reviewing ongoing program activities in order to determine if the program is being implemented as planned.

040201   Sources of social, physical, political, cultural, and economic information.
040202   Characteristics of valid and reliable data-gathering instruments.
040203   Health risk appraisals.
040204   Psychosocial assessment instruments.
040224   Application of evaluations.

0403   Monitor the health education program by comparing results with outcome criteria in order to determine program effectiveness.

040301   Sources of social, physical, political, cultural, and economic information.
040302   Characteristics of valid and reliable data-gathering instruments.
040303   Health risk appraisals.
040304   Psychosocial assessment instruments.
040324   Application of evaluations.

0404   Modify the health education program as indicated by comparison of results with criteria in order to enhance the likelihood of program success.

      040401   Sources of social, physical, political, cultural, and economic information.
      040402   Characteristics of valid and reliable data-gathering instruments.
      040403   Health risk appraisals.
      040404   Psychosocial assessment instruments.
      040424   Application of evaluations.

05 COORDINATE PROVISION OF HEALTH EDUCATION SERVICES

0501   Elicit the cooperation of persons from diverse programs by establishing relationships with and between those individuals in order to coordinate related health education services.

      050110   Communication techniques.
      050111   Methods of reporting data.
      050112   Strategies for identifying and involving community organizations, resources, and participants.
      050113   Social, cultural, and political structures.
      050114   Practical modes of collaboration.
      050115   Group dynamics.
      050116   Strategies for dealing with controversial health issues.
      050122   Program management techniques and principles.
      050125   Methods of conflict resolution (e.g., negotiations, confrontation).
      050134   Characteristics of different organizations (e.g., public, voluntary, professional).
      050138   Roles of health and related professionals.

06 ACT AS A RESOURCE PERSON IN HEALTH EDUCATION

0601   Select sources of information on health issues by evaluating these sources in order to disseminate health information to individuals and/or groups.

      060101   Sources of social, physical, political, cultural, and economic information.
      060102   Characteristics of valid and reliable data-gathering information.
      060105   Physical, social, emotional, and intellectual factors.
      060106   Behaviors that tend to promote or compromise health.
      060107   Theories underlying change.
      060108   Available health education services.
      060126   Professional literature, including current research, trends, issues, and professional associations and organizations.
      060127   Organizations and agencies that provide various types of health information, health services and expertise.
      060128   Ways to evaluate the worth and applicability of resource materials for given audiences.
      060129   Different methods for distributing educational materials.
      060130   Processes for acquiring resource materials.
      060131   Approaches for referring requests to valid sources of health information.

060132 General processes for identifying the information needed to satisfy a request.

0602 Serve as a consultant to individuals and groups by assisting in the identification of issues and recommending alternative strategies in order to meet their needs.

060208 Available health education services.
060209 Gaps and overlaps in the provision of collaborative health services.
060210 Communication techniques.
060212 Strategies for identifying and involving community organizations, resources, and participants.
060213 Social, cultural, and political structures.
060214 Practical modes of collaboration.
060215 Group dynamics.
060216 Strategies for dealing with controversial health issues.
060217 The importance of societal value systems.
060223 Strategies for conducting in-service training programs.
060236 Code of ethics of the profession.

07 COMMUNICATE HEALTH AND HEALTH EDUCATION NEEDS, CONCERNS, AND RESOURCES

0701 Keep abreast of professional literature, current trends, and research by reviewing literature and attending professional meetings in order to maintain knowledge and skills.

070101 Sources of social, physical, political, cultural, and economic information.
070121 Educational resources and criteria for selection.
070126 Professional literature, including current research, trends, issues, and professional associations and organizations.
070137 Statistical techniques and terms.

0702 Advocate for the inclusion of health education in health programs and services.

070210 Communication techniques.
070212 Strategies for identifying and involving community organizations, resources, and participants.
070213 Social, cultural, and political structures.
070214 Practical modes of collaboration.
070215 Group dynamics.
070225 Methods of conflict resolution (e.g., negotiations, confrontation).
070233 Legislative process.
070234 Characteristics of different organizations (e.g., public, voluntary, professional).
070238 Roles of health and related professionals.

0703   Explain the foundations of the discipline of health education including its purposes, theories, history, ethics, and contributions in order to promote the development and practice of health education.

    070307   Theories underlying change.
    070326   Professional literature, including current research, trends, issues, and professional associations and organizations.
    070335   State of the art of health education as a profession.
    070336   Code of ethics of the profession.

0704   Select communication methods and techniques by matching characteristics of individual/target group with methods/techniques and issues in order to assess, plan, implement, and evaluate health education services.

    070405   Physical, social, emotional, and intellectual factors.
    070406   Behaviors that tend to promote or compromise health.
    070407   Theories underlying change.
    070411   Methods of reporting data.
    070410   Communication techniques.

A P P E N D I X   T H R E E

Answers to Key Practice Questions

Context
(page 1)

1-a; 2-c; 3-b; 4-d; 5-d; 6-c; 7-d; 8-a; 9-a; 10-a; 11-c; 12-a; 13-b

I. Assessing Needs
(page 21)

1-a; 2-d; 3-d; 4-b; 5-c; 6-a

II. Planning
(page 31)

1-a; 2-c; 3-a; 4-b; 5-a; 6-c; 7-a; 8-b; 9-c; 10-d

III. Implementing
(page 43)

1-d; 2-d; 3-b; 4-c

IV. Evaluating
(page 51)

1-b; 2-a; 3-c; 4-a; 5-b; 6-a; 7-a

V. Coordinating
(page 59)

1-d; 2-d

VI. Acting As A Resource
(page 61)

1-a; 2-d; 3-a; 4-c

VII. Communicating
(page 67)

1-b; 2-b; 3-a; 4-c

School
(page 81)

1-d; 2-a; 3-c; 4-b; 5-c; 6-b

Community
(page 85)

1-b; 2-a; 3-d; 4-a; 5-d; 6-c

Worksite
(page 91)

1-d; 2-b; 3-b; 4-d; 5-d

Health Care
(page 93)

1-a; 2-b; 3-c; 4-b

REFERENCES FOR INTRODUCTION AND CONTEXT

Bracht, Neil F., ed. Health Promotion at the Community Level. Newbury Park, CA: Sage Publications, 1990.

CCLDHE Calif, Conf. of Local Directors of Health Education. Standards of Practice for Public Health Education in CA Local Health Departments. CCLDHE, 1991.

Courtenay, Bradley. "Are Psychological Models of Adult Development Still Important for the Practice of Adult Education?" Adult Education Quarterly 44 (3)1994: 145-152.

Green, L.W. "Determining the Impact and Effectiveness of Health Education as It Relates to Federal Policy." Health Education Monographs 6 (Supplement)1978.

Green, Lawrence W. and Marshall W. Kreuter. Health Promotion Planning: An Educational and Environmental Approach. 2nd ed., Mountain View, CA: Mayberry, 1991.

McKenzie, J.F. and R.R. Pringer. Introduction to Community Health. Sudbury, MA: Jones & Bartlett Publishers, 1997.

Minkler, Meredith. "Ethical Issues in Community Organization." Health Education Monographs 6 (3) 1978.

NCHEC. A Competency-Based Framework for Professional Development of Certified Health Education Specialists. Allentown, PA: The National Commission for Health Education Credentialing, Inc., 1996.

Pickett, George and John Hanlon. Public Health Administration and Practice. St. Louis, MO: Times Mirror/Mosby, 1990.

Pollock, Marion. "Private communication on school health education." 1992.

Torjman, P. Prevention in the Drug Field: Essential Concepts and Strategies. Toronto, Canada: Addiction Research Foundation, 1986.

USDHHS, PHS. Healthy People 2000: National Health Promotion & Disease Prevention Objectives. US Dept. of Health & Human Services, Public Health Service: Office of the Secretary for Health, Washington, D.C., 1990. DHHS Pub. No. (PHS) 91-50212.

I. REFERENCES FOR ASSESSING NEEDS

Breitose, P. Focus Groups — When and How to Use Them: A Practical Guide. Health Promotion Resource Center, Stanford University School of Medicine, Palo Alto, CA, 1988.

Breckon, Donald J., John R. Harvey, and R. Brick Lancaster. Community Health Education: Settings, Roles, and Skills for the 21st Century. 3rd ed., Gaithersburg, MD: Aspen Publications, 1994.

Cross, T. L., B. J. Bazron, K. W. Dennis, and M. R. Isaacs. Towards a Culturally Competent System of Care: A Monograph on Effective Services for Minority Children Who Are Severely Emotionally Disturbed. Georgetown University Child Development Center, CASSP Technical Assistance Center, 1989.

DeFriese, Gordon H. and Jonathan E. Fielding. "Health Risk Appraisal in the 1990's: Opportunities, Challenges, Expectations." In Annual Review of Public Health, 401-418. 11, 1990.

Delbecq, A.L. "The Nominal Group as a Technique for Understanding the Qualitative Dimensions of Client Needs." In Assessing Health and Human Service Needs, ed. R.A. et al. Bell. New York: Human Sciences Press, 1983.

Dever, G.E. Alan. Community Health Analysis: Global Awareness at the Local Level. 2nd ed., Gaithersburg, MD: Aspen Publications, 1991.

Dignan, M.B. and P.A. Carr. Program Planning for Health Education and Health Promotion. Philadelphia, PA: Lea & Febinger, 1987.

Gilmore, G.D., M.D. Campbell, and B.L. Becker. Needs Assessment Strategies for Health Education and Health Promotion. Indianapolis, IN: Benchmark, 1989.

Gordon, N. So You're Thinking About Conducting A Survey... Oakland, CA: Kaiser Permanente Div. of Research, 1990.

Wagner, Laura N. Writing Effective Survey Questions. Health Promotion Resource Center, Stanford U. School of Medicine, Palo Alto, CA, 1993.

II. REFERENCES FOR PLANNING EFFECTIVE PROGRAMS

Breckon, Donald J., John R. Harvey, and R. Brick Lancaster. Community Health Education: Settings, Roles, and Skills for the 21st Century. 3rd ed., Gaithersburg, MD: Aspen Publications, 1994.

Bryson, John M. Strategic Planning for Public and Nonprofit Organizations. 2nd ed., San Francisco, CA: Jossey-Bass, 1995.

Calif. Conf. of Local Directors of Health Education. Standards of Practice for Public Health Education in CA Local Health Departments. CCLDHE, 1991.

CDC. Planned Approach to Community Health: Guide for the Local Coordinator. Natl. Ctr. for Chronic Disease Prevention & Health Promotion. CDCP, Atlanta, GA.

Duhl, L.J. "An Ecohistory of Health: The Role of Healthy Cities." American Journal of Health Promotion 10 (4)1996: 258-261.

Fodor, J.T., G.T. Dalis, and S.C. Giarratano. Health Instruction. 5th ed., Baltimore, MD: Williams & Wilkins, 1995.

Green, Lawrence W., Marshall W. Kreuter, Sigrid G. Deeds, and Kaye B. Partridge. Health Education Planning: A Diagnostic Approach. Palo Alto, CA: Mayfield, 1980.

Green, Lawrence W. and Marshall W. Kreuter. Health Promotion Planning: An Educational and Environmental Approach. 2nd ed., Mountain View, CA: Mayfield, 1991.

Krueter, Marshall W., N.A. Lezin, and L.W. Green. Community Health Promotion Ideas That Work. Sudbury, MA: Jones & Bartlett Publishers, 1998.

Rogers, Everett. Diffusion of Innovation. New York: Free Press, 1983.

Ross, M.G. and B.W. Lappin. Community Organization: Theory, Practice and Principles. 2nd ed., New York: Harper Rowe, 1967.

Simons-Morton, Bruce, Walter Greene, and Nell Gottlieb. Introduction to Health Education. 2nd ed., Prospect Heights, IL: Waveland Press, 1995.

USDHHS, PHS. Healthy People 2000: National Health Promotion & Disease Prevention Objectives. US Dept. of Health & Human Services, Public Health Service: Office of the Secretary for Health, Washington, D.C., 1990. DHHS Pub. No. (PHS) 91-50212.

WHO. Twenty Steps for Developing a Healthy Cities Project. WHO Regional Office for Europe, Copenhagen, Denmark, 1992.

Zais, R.S. Curriculum Principles and Foundations. New York: Thomas Y. Crowell Company, Inc., 1990.

III. REFERENCES FOR IMPLEMENTING PROGRAMS

The Survey Kit. Thousand Oaks, CA: Sage, 1995.

Calif. Conf. of Local Directors of Health Education. Standards of Practice for Public Health Education in CA Local Health Departments. CCLDHE, 1991.

Forouzesh, M. Unpublished notes. 1991.

AAHE, American Association for Health Education. "Code of Ethics for Health Educators." Journal of Health Education 25 (4) 1944: 197-200.

Breitose, P. Focus Groups — When and How to Use Them: A Practical Guide. Health Promotion Resource Center, Stanford University School of Medicine, Palo Alto, CA, 1988.

Dalis, G. T. "Effective Health Instruction: Both a Science and an Art." Journal of Health Education 25 (5) 1994: 289-294.

Doak, Cecilia C., Leonard G. Doak, and Jane H. Root. Teaching Patients with Low-Literacy Skills. 2nd ed., Philadelphia, PA: J.B. Lippincott, 1995.

Faden, Ruth R. and Allen J. Faden. "The Ethics of Health Education as Public Policy." Health Education Monographs 12 (3) 1985:

Giloth, B.E., ed. Managing Hospital-Based Patient Education. Chicago, IL: American Hospital Association, 1993.

Meeks, L., P. Heit, and R.M. Page. Comprehensive School Health Education: Totally Awesome Strategies for Teaching Health. Blacklick, OH: MeeksHeit, 1996.

Minkler, Meredith. "Ethical Issues in Community Organization." Health Education Monographs 6 (3) 1978:

Simons-Morton, Bruce, Walter Greene, and Nell Gottlieb. Introduction to Health Education. 2nd ed., Prospect Heights, IL: Waveland Press, 1995.

Wilson, B. A. and T. E. Glaros. Managing Health Promotion Programs. Champaign, IL: Human Kinetics, 1994.

IV. REFERENCES FOR EVALUATING EFFECTIVENESS OF PROGRAMS

Glanz, Karen, Frances Marcus Lewis, and Barbara K. Rimer, ed. <u>Health Behavior and Health Education: Theory, Research & Practice.</u> 1st ed., San Francisco, CA: Jossey-Bass, 1990.

Green, Lawrence W. and Francis M. Lewis. <u>Measurement and Evaluation in Health Education and Health Promotion.</u> Mountain View, CA: Mayfield, 1986.

Herman, Joan, ed. <u>Program Evaluation Kit.</u> Thousand Oaks, CA: Sage, 1987. *This kit includes nine separate "how-to" volumes.*

Mohr, Lawrence. <u>Impact Analysis for Program Evaluation.</u> Thousand Oaks, CA: Sage, 1995.

Pelletier, K. R. "A Review and Analysis of the Health and Cost-effective Outcome Studies of Comprehensive Health Promotion and Disease Prevention Programs at the Worksite." <u>American Journal of Health Promotion</u> 8,1993: 50-62.

Posevac, E.M. and R.G. Carey. <u>Program Evaluation: Methods and Studies.</u> 4th ed., Englewood Cliffs, NJ: Prentice Hall, 1994.

<u>The Survey Kit.</u> Thousand Oaks, CA: Sage, 1995. *This series of nine volumes covers all basic aspects of surveying. Each volume can be purchased separately.*

Simons-Morton, Bruce, Walter Greene, and Nell Gottlieb. <u>Introduction to Health Education.</u> 2nd ed., Prospect Heights, IL: Waveland Press, 1995.

Tones, K., S. Tilford, and Y. Robinson, ed. <u>Health Education: Effectiveness and Efficiency.</u> London: Chapman and Hall, 1991.

Wagner, Laura N. <u>Writing Effective Survey Questions.</u> Health Promotion Resource Center, Stanford U. School of Medicine, Palo Alto, CA, 1993.

Windsor, R.A., T. Baranowski, N. Clark, and G. Cutter. <u>Evaluation of Health Promotion, Health Education, and Disease Prevention Programs.</u> 2nd ed., Mountain View, CA: Mayfield, 1994.

V. REFERENCES FOR COORDINATING PROVISION OF SERVICES

Beresford, T. <u>How to Be a Trainer.</u> Baltimore, MD: Planned Parenthood of Maryland, 1980.

Breckon, Donald J., John R. Harvey, and R. Brick Lancaster. <u>Community Health Education: Settings, Roles, and Skills for the 21st Century.</u> 3rd ed., Gaithersburg, MD: Aspen Publications, 1994.

<u>Building and Maintaining Coalitions.</u> Health Promotion Resource Center, Stanford Center for Research in Disease Prevention, 1990.

Simons-Morton, Bruce, Walter Greene, and Nell Gottlieb. <u>Introduction to Health Education.</u> 2nd ed., Prospect Heights, IL: Waveland Press, 1995.

VI. REFERENCES FOR ACTING AS A RESOURCE PERSON

Breckon, Donald J., John R. Harvey, and R. Brick Lancaster. <u>Community Health Education: Settings, Roles, and Skills for the 21st Century.</u> 3rd ed., Gaithersburg, MD: Aspen Publications, 1994.

Dalis, G. T. "Effective Health Instruction: Both a Science and an Art." <u>Journal of Health Education</u> 25 (5) 1994: 289-294.

Ferguson, Tom. <u>Health Online: How to Find Health Information, Support Groups, and Self-Help Communities in Cyberspace.</u> Reading, PA: Addison-Wesley, 1996.

Fodor, J.T., G.T. Dalis, and S.C. Giarratano. <u>Health Instruction.</u> 5th ed., Baltimore, MD: Williams & Wilkins, 1995.

Gold, Robert. <u>Microcomputer Applications in Health Education.</u> Dubuque, IA: William C. Brown, 1991.

Harris, Linda, ed. <u>Health and the New Media: Technologies Transforming Personal and Public Health.</u> Lawrence Erlbaum Associates, 1995.

Leonard, Janet. <u>Interacting: Multimedia and Health.</u> London: Hamilton House, Mabledon Place, London WC1H9TX, 1994.

Lieberman, D. "Computers' Potential Role in Health Education." <u>Health Communication</u> 4 (33) 1992: 211-225.

Lippitt, G. and R. Lippitt. <u>The Consulting Process in Action.</u> San Diego, CA: University Associates, 1978.

Stivers, C., M.K. Bentley, and L.L. Meccouri. "Internet: The Contemporary Health Educator's Most Versatile Tool." <u>Journal of Health Education</u> 26 (4) 1995:

VII. REFERENCES FOR COMMUNICATING HEALTH EDUCATION

Andreasen, Alan R. <u>Marketing Social Change: Changing Behavior to Promote Health, Social Development, and the Environment.</u> San Francisco, CA: Jossey-Bass, 1995.

ASTDHPPHE. <u>Roles and Functions of Health Promotion and Health Education Units in State Health Departments.</u> Assoc. of State & Territorial Directors of Hlth. Promo. & Pub. Hlth. Education.

Atkin, Charles and Lawrence Wallack, ed. <u>Mass Communication and Public Health.</u> Newbury Park, CA: Sage Publications, 1990.

Flora, J.A., E. Maibach, and N. Maccoby. "The Role of Mass Media in Health Promotion." In <u>Annual Review of Public Health</u>, ed. L. Breslow. Palo Alto, CA: Annual Reviews, 1989.

Glanz, Karen, Frances Marcus Lewis, and Barbara K. Rimer, ed. <u>Health Behavior and Health Education: Theory, Research & Practice.</u> San Francisco, CA: Jossey-Bass, 1990.

Green, Lawrence W. "Determining the Impact and Effectiveness of Health Education as it Relates to Federal Policy." <u>Health Education Monographs</u> 6 (Supplement 1), 1978: 28-66.

Green, Lawrence W. and A. McAlister. "Macro-Intervention to Support Health Behavior: Some Theoretical Perspectives and Practical Reflections." <u>Health Education Quarterly</u> 11 (3) 1984: 322-339.

Green, Lawrence W. and Marshall W. Kreuter. <u>Health Promotion Planning: An Educational and Environmental Approach.</u> 2nd ed., Mountain View, CA: Mayfield, 1991.

Harris, Linda, ed. <u>Health and the New Media: Technologies Transforming Personal and Public Health.</u> Lawrence Erlbaum Associates, 1995.

Kotler, P. and A. R. Andreasen. <u>Strategic Marketing for Nonprofit Organizations.</u> Englewood Cliffs, NJ: Prentice Hall, 1987.

Marcus, Bess H., Bernardine M. Pinto, Laurey R. Simkin, Janet E. Audrain, and Elaine R. Taylor. "Application of Theoretical Models to Exercise Behavior Among Employed Women." <u>American Journal of Health Promotion</u> 9 (1) 1994: 49-55.

McGuire, W, J. "Theoretical Foundations for Campaigns." In <u>Public Communications Campaigns</u>, ed. R.E. Rice and C.K. Atkin. Newbury Park, CA: Sage, 1990.

NCI, DHHS. <u>Media Strategies for Smoking Control.</u> Consensus Workshop by the Advocacy Institute, 1988.

Steckler, Allen, et al. "Health Intervention Strategies: Recommendations for Future Research." <u>HEQ</u> 22 (3) 1995:

Stiff, James B. <u>Persuasive Communication.</u> New York: Guilford, 1994.

Wilder, Claudyne. <u>The Presentations Kit: Ten Steps to Selling Your Ideas.</u> New York: Wiley, 1990.

REFERENCES FOR THEORIES AND MODELS OF BEHAVIOR CHANGE

Glaser, B.G., and A.L. Strauss. <u>The Discovery of Grounded Theory: Strategies for Qualitative Research.</u> Chicago: Aldine-Atherton, 1967.

Green, L.W., and M.W. Kreuter. <u>Health Promotion Planning: An Educational and Environmental Approach.</u> 2nd ed., Mountain View, CA: Mayfield, 1991.

Green, L.W., M.W. Kreuter, S.G. Deeds, and K.B. Partridge. <u>Health Education Planning: A Diagnostic Approach.</u> Mountain View, CA: Mayfield, 1980.

Lewin, K. "Field Theory in Social Science." <u>Selected Theoretical Papers.</u> ed. D. Cartwright. New York: Harper & Row, 1951.

Maslow, A.H. <u>Toward a Psychology of Being.</u> 2nd ed., New York: Van Nostrand Reinhold, 1968.

Mullen, P.D., and R. Reynolds. "The Potential of Grounded Theory for Health Education Research: Linking Theory and Practice." <u>Health Education Monographs</u> 6: 280-294.

INDIVIDUAL CHANGE MODELS

Ajzen, I., and M. Fishbein. <u>Understanding Attitudes and Predicting Social Behavior.</u> Englewood Cliffs, NJ: Prentice Hall, 1980.

Bandura, A. <u>Social Foundations of Thought and Action: A Social Cognitive Theory.</u> Englewood Cliffs, NJ: Prentice Hall, 1986.

Bandura, A. <u>Social Learning Theory.</u> Englewood Cliffs, NJ: Prentice Hall, 1977.

Becker, M.H., and I.M. Rosenstock. "Comparing Social Learning Theory and the Health Belief Model." In <u>Advances in Health Education and Promotion.</u> Vol. 2. ed. W.B. Ward. Greenwich, CT: JAI Press, 1987 (245-249).

Diclemente, C.C., and J.O. Prochaska. "Process and Stages of Self-Change: Coping and Competence in Smoking Behavior Change." In Coping and Substance Use. eds. Shiffman and Wills. Orlando, FL: Academic Press, 1985.

Fishbein, M., and I. Ajzen. Belief, Attitude, Intention and Behavior. Reading, MA: Addison-Wesley, 1975.

Gottlieb, B. Social Networks and Social Support. Newbury Park, CA: Sage, 1981.

Janz, N.K., and M.H. Becker. "The Health Belief Model: A Decade Later." Health Education Quarterly 11 (1984): 1-47.

Maslow, A.H. Hierarchy of Needs.

Mecca, A.M., N.J. Smelser, and J. Vasconcellos. The Social Importance of Self-Esteem. Berkeley, CA: University of California Press, 1989.

Minkler, M.M. "Applications of Social Support Theory to Health Education: Implications for Work With Elderly." Health Education Quarterly 8 (1981): 147-165.

Pomerleau O.F., and J.P. Brady. Behavioral Medicine: Theory and Practice. Baltimore, MD: Williams & Wilkins, 1979.

Rosenstock, I.M., V.J. Stretcher, and M.H. Becker. "Social Learning Theory and the Health Belief Model." Health Education Quarterly 15, no. 2 (1988): 175-183.

Skinner, B.F. About Behaviorism. New York: Knopf, 1974.

Stretcher, V.J., B.M. Devellis, M.H. Becker, and I.M. Rosenstock. "The Role of Self-Efficacy in Achieving Health Behavior Change." Health Education Quarterly 13 (1986): 73-91.

Wallston, K.S., and B.N. Wallston. "Health locus of control." Health Education Monographs 6, no. 2 (Spring 1978): 101-170.

Wallston, K.S., and B.N. Wallston. "Who is responsible for your health? The Construct of Health Locus of Control." In Social Psychology of Health and Illness eds. G. Sanders and J. Suls. Hillsdale, NJ: Lawrence Erlbaum Assoc., 1982: 65-95.

COMMUNICATION THEORIES AND MODELS

Defleur, M.L., and S. Ball-Rokeach. Theories of Mass Communication, 1989.

Festinger, L. <u>A Theory of Cognitive Dissonance.</u> Stanford, CA: Stanford University Press, 1962.

Green, L.W., and A.L. McAlister. "Macro Intervention to Support Health Behavior: Some Theoretical Perspectives and Practical Reflections." <u>Health Education Quarterly</u> 2, no. 3. 1984: 323-339.

Hovland, C.I., I.L. Janis, and H.H. Kelly. <u>Communications and Persuasion.</u> New Haven, CT: Yale University Press, 1953.

McGuire, W. "Theoretical Foundations of Public Communications Campaigns." In <u>Public Communications Campaigns.</u> eds. Rice and Paisley. Newbury Park, CA: Sage, 1981, 41-70.

Rank, H. "Teaching About Public Persuasion." In <u>Teaching About Doublespeak.</u> ed. D. Dietrich. Urbana, IL: National Council of Teachers of English, 1976.

COMMUNITY LEVEL

Berlo, D.K. <u>The Process of Communication.</u> New York: Holt, Rinehart & Winston, 1960.

Rogers, E.S. <u>The Diffusion of Innovation.</u> New York: Free Press, 1983.

Rothman, J. "Three Models of Community Organization Practice." In <u>Strategies of Communication Organization.</u> ed. F.M. Cos, et al. 3rd ed., Peacock, F.E., 1979.

SCHOOL SETTINGS

Allensworth, D.D. "Health Education:State of the Art." <u>Journal of School Health</u> 63 (1) 1993: 14-20.

Allensworth, D. D. "The Research Base For Innovative Practices in School Health Education at The Secondary Level." <u>Journal of School Health</u> 64 (5) 1994: 180-187.

Allensworth, D.D. and L.J. Kolbe. "The Comprehensive School Health Program: Exploring an Expanded Concept." <u>Journal of School Health</u> 57 (10) 1987: 409-413.

Ames, E.E., L.A. Trucano, J.C. Wan, and M.H. Harris. <u>Designing School Health Curricula.</u> 2nd ed., Dubuque, IA: W.C. Brown, 1995.

Carnegie. <u>Turning Points: Preparing American Youth for the 21st Century.</u> Washington, DC: Carnegie Council on Adolescent Development, 1989.

Cortese, Peter and K. Middleton, ed. <u>The Comprehensive School Health Challenge: Promoting Health Through Education.</u> Santa Cruz, CA: ETR Associates, 1994.

Creswell, W.H. and I.M. Newman. <u>School Health Practice.</u> 10th ed., St. Louis, MO: Mosby, 1993.

Dalis, G. T. "Effective Health Instruction: Both a Science and an Art." <u>Journal of Health Education</u> 25 (5)1994: 289-294.

English, J. "Innovative Practices in Comprehensive Health Education for Elementary Schools." <u>Journal of School Health</u> 64 (5) 1994: 188-191.

Fodor, J.T., G.T. Dalis, and S.C. Giarratano. <u>Health Instruction.</u> 5th ed., Baltimore, MD: Williams & Wilkins, 1995.

JCNHES — Joint Committee on National Health Education Standards. <u>National Health Education Standards: Achieving Health Literacy.</u> American Cancer Society, Atlanta, GA, 1995.

Kane, W.M. <u>Step by Step to Comprehensive School Health.</u> Santa Cruz, CA: ETR Associates, 1993.

Kolbe, Lloyd J., Laura Kann, Janet L. Collins, et al. "The School Health Policies and Program Study (SHPPS): Context, Methods, General Findings, and Future Efforts." <u>Journal of School Health</u> 65 (8) 1995: 339-343.

Meeks, L., P. Heit, and R.M. Page. <u>Comprehensive School Health Education: Totally Awesome Strategies for Teaching Health.</u> Blacklick, OH: MeeksHeit, 1996.

Metropolitan Life. <u>Health: You've Got to be Taught: An Evaluation of Comprehensive Health Education in American Public Schools.</u> New York: Metropolitan Life Foundation, 1988.

NASBE, Nat. Assoc. of State Boards of Education. <u>Code Blue: Uniting for Healthier Youth.</u> The National Commission on the Role of the School and the Community in Improving Adolescent Health, 1990.

Pollock, M.B. and K. Middleton. <u>School Health Instruction.</u> 3rd ed., St. Louis, MO: Mosby, 1994.

Potter, P. and A. Perry. "Fundamentals of Learning." In <u>Mosby YearBook</u>, St Louis, MO: Mosby, 1993.

Zais, R.S. <u>Curriculum Principles and Foundations.</u> New York: Thomas Y. Crowell Company, Inc., 1990.

COMMUNITY SETTINGS

Healthy People 2000: National Health Promotion & Disease Prevention Objectives. Washington, D.C.: DHHS Pub. No. (PHS) 91-502-12, 1990.

Healthy Communities 2000: Model Standards, Guidelines for Community Attainment of the Year 2000 National Health Objectives. Washington, D.C.: American Public Health Association, 1991.

Andreasen, Alan R. Marketing Social Change: Changing Behavior to Promote Health, Social Development, and the Environment. San Francisco, CA: Jossey-Bass, 1995.

Bracht, Neil F., ed. Health Promotion at the Community Level. Newbury Park, CA: Sage Publications, 1990.

Freudenberg, Nichollas, Eugenia Eng, Byron Flay, et al. "Strengthening Individual and Community Capacity to Prevent Disease and Promote Health in Search of Relevant Theories and Principles." Health Education Quarterly 22 (3) 1995: 290-306.

Jackson, C., D.G. Altman, B. Howard-Pitney, and J.W. Farquhar. "Evaluating Community-Level Health Promotion and Disease Prevention Interventions." In Evaluating Health Promotion Programs, ed. Marc T. Braverman. San Francisco, CA: Jossey Bass, 1989.

Minkler, Meredith. "Improving Health Through Community Organization." In Health Behavior and Health Education: Theory, Research and Practice, ed. K. Glanz, F.M. Lewis, and B.K. Rimer. San Francisco, CA: Jossey Bass, 1990.

Parcel, Guy S., Cheryl L. Perry, and Wendell C. Taylor. "Beyond Demonstration: Diffusion of Health Promotion Innovations." In Health Promotion at the Community Level, ed. Neil Bracht. Newbury Park, CA: Sage, 1990.

Rogers, Everett. Diffusion of Innovation. New York: Free Press, 1983.

Ross, M.G. and B.W. Lappin. Community Organization: Theory, Practice and Principles. 2nd ed., New York: Harper Rowe, 1967.

Rothman, J. "Three Models of Community Organization Practice." In Strategies of Community Organization, ed. F. M. Cox. Itasca, IL: Peacock, 1974.

Simons-Morton, Bruce, Walter Greene, and Nell Gottlieb. Introduction to Health Education. 2nd ed., Prospect Heights, IL: Waveland Press, 1995.

Wallerstein, Nina and E. Bernstein. "Introduction to Community Empowerment, Participatory Education, and Health." Health Education Quarterly 21, 1994: 141-148.

WHO. Twenty Steps for Developing a Healthy Cities Project. WHO Regional Office for Europe, Copenhagen, Denmark, 1992.

WORKSITE SETTINGS

Chenoweth, D. H. Planning Health Promotion at the Worksite. Indianapolis, IN: Benchmark,1987.

DeFriese, Gordon H. and Jonathan E. Fielding. "Health Risk Appraisal in the 1990's: Opportunities, Challenges, Expectations." In Annual Review of Public Health, 401-418. 1l, 1990.

DeJoy, D. M. and D.J. Southern. "An Integrative Perspective on Worksite Health Promotion." Journal of Occupational Medicine 35 1993: 1221-1230.

DeJoy, D. M. and M. G. Wilson. Critical Issues in Worksite Health Promotion. Boston: Allyn and Bacom, 1995.

Heirich, M. A., J.C. Erfurt, and A. Foote. "The Core Technology of Worksite Wellness." Journal of Occupational Medicine 34 1992: 627-637.

Kozier, B., G. Erb, K. Blaise, and J. Wildinson, ed. Concepts and Issues in Nursing Practice. Redwood City, CA: Addison-Wesley, 1995.

Marcus, Bess H., Bernardine M. Pinto, Laurey R. Simkin, Janet E. Audrain, and Elaine R. Taylor. "Application of Theoretical Models to Exercise Behavior Among Employed Women." American Journal of Health Promotion 9 (1) 1994: 49-55.

O'Donnell, M.P. and J.S. Harris. Health Promotion in the Workplace. 2nd ed., Albany, NY: Delmar, 1994.

Pelletier, K.R. "A Review and Analysis of the Health and Cost-effective Outcome Studies of Comprehensive Health Promotion and Disease Prevention Programs at the Worksite." American Journal of Health Promotion 8, 1993: 50-62.

Ramirez, S. Health Promotion for All: Strategies for Reaching Diverse Populations at the Worksite. 1994.

Sorensen, G., J.S. Himmelstein, and M.K. Hunt. "A Model for Worksite Cancer Prevention: Integration of Health Protection and Health Promotion in the Wellworks Project." American Journal of Health Promotion 10 1995: 55-62.

Wilson, B.A. and T.E. Glaros. Managing Health Promotion Programs. Champaign, IL: Human Kinetics, 1994.

Wilson, M.G., P.B. Holman, and A. Hammock. "Examining The Effects of Comprehensive Worksite Health Promotion Using The Business Responds to AIDS Framework." American Journal of Health Promotion (In press)

HEALTH-CARE SETTINGS

CDC. "Prevention and Managed Care: Opportunities for Managed Care Organizations, Purchasers of Health Care, and Public Health Agencies." Morbidity & Mortality Weekly 44, 1995: RR-14.

Deeds, S.G., B.J. Hebert, and J.M. Wolle. A Model for Patient Education Programming. Washington, D.C.: American Public Health Association, 1979.

Doak, Cecilia C., Leonard G. Doak, and Jane H. Root. Teaching Patients with Low-Literacy Skills. 2nd ed., Philadelphia, PA: J.B. Lippincott, 1995.

Giloth, B.E., ed. Managing Hospital-Based Patient Education. Chicago, IL: American Hospital Association, 1993.

Improving Adherence Among Hypertensive Patients: The Physician's Guide. USDHHS NHLBI, March, 1987.

Kozier, B., G. Erb, K. Blaise, and J. Wildinson, ed. Concepts and Issues in Nursing Practice. Redwood City, CA: Addison-Wesley, 1995.

Lorig, K. Patient Education: A Practical Approach. St. Louis, MO: Mosby Year Book, Inc., 1991.

Mielke, Danny R. "Health Services for Health Educators." Journal of Health Education 225 (4) 1994: 218-222.

Redman, Barbara. The Process of Patient Education. Mosby Yearbook, St. Louis, MO: Mosby, 1993.

About The Contributors

Michael J. Cleary, Ed.D., CHES

Dr. Cleary is a professor in the Department of Allied Health at Slippery Rock University where he coordinates the School Health Program as well as the Graduate Program. Dr. Cleary previously taught health education and driver education at Evanston Township High School in Evanston, Illinois and later served as the lead teacher specialist at the McMillen Center for Health Education in Fort Wayne, Indiana. Currently a member of the Division Board for Professional Preparation, he has written and presented widely on performance-based assessments in both community health and school health professional preparation programs.

Brad Neiger, Ph.D., CHES

Dr. Neiger is an associate professor of health education at Brigham Young University. He has also directed health education programs at a state health department, a county health department and for managed health care organization. He has taught at the University of Utah and Utah State University. Dr. Neiger has served as the vice-chair of the National Commission for Health Education Credentialing and as the chair of its Division Board for Professional Preparation. He has also served as president of the Health Education Association of Utah. He has extensive experience in community health education settings, planning and evaluation, policy development and legislation, curriculum development, and social marketing.

Kathleen Middleton, M.S., CHES

Ms. Middleton is currently director and publisher for ToucanEd Publications and Communications. She has a variety of experiences in health education which include teaching health in a public school classroom setting and to prosepctive teachers in five different universities in California. She has administered health and prevention programs for the Monterey County Office of Education and served as the director of school health for the National Center for Health Education. Her experience in materials development is extensive, having authored and edited hundreds of books, textbooks, curricula, articles and educational brochures for health education. She served as editor-in-chief for ETR Associates, where she coordinated and edited numerous projects including the Comprehensive School Health Challenge (with Dr. Peter A. Cortese). (1994, ETR Associates) Ms. Middleton has served on boards of directors for a variety of professional associations including the American Association for Health Education (AAHE). Currently, she serves the National Commission for Health Education Credentialing, Inc. on the Division Board for Professional Preparation and as a commissioner.